The Courage to be Chaste

also by Benedict Groeschel
published by Paulist Press

Listening at Prayer (book)

Learning the Art of Prayer (cassette program)
Learning to Pray in the Life of the Spirit
The Road to Recollection and Inner Peace
The Divine Readings—Prayer with Scripture
The Divine Liturgy—Prayer with Christ
Contemplative Meditation—The Inner Music
The Prayer of Life—Praying Always
The Contemplative Way—Preparing for God's Gift

Adventures on the Spiritual Journey (cassette program)
The Longest Journey: The Spiritual Journey Within
The Call of God—Beginning Every Day
Growing Integration and Purity of Heart
Overcoming Obstacles to Spiritual Growth—in Mind and Heart
Darkness and Its Uses for Self and Others
The Illumination—The Work and Prayer of Enlightenment
The Goal—Union and Peace While Waiting for God

God and Us (cassette program)
Our Creation and Being
Our Fall into Darkness—The Incarnate God
The Passion and Resurrection
Our Healing and Hope—The Holy Spirit
Our Mother—The Church
Our Eternal Destiny—Life After Death

THE COURAGE
TO BE CHASTE

Benedict J. Groeschel, C.F.R.

Paulist Press
New York/Mahwah

Nihil Obstat:
Daniel V. Flynn, J.C.D.
Censor Librorum

Imprimatur:
Joseph T. O'Keefe,
Vicar General, Archdiocese of New York

February 27, 1985

The Nihil Obstat and Imprimatur are official declarations that a book or pamphlet is free of doctrinal or moral error. No implication is contained therein that those who have granted the Nihil Obstat and Imprimatur agree with the contents, opinions or statements expressed.

Library of Congress
Catalog Card Number: 85-60295

ISBN: 0-8091-2705-9

Published by Paulist Press
997 Macarthur Boulevard
Mahwah, New Jersey 07430

Printed and bound in the United States of America

Contents

The Book Is Dedicated to
the Men and Women of Courage
and to all who have the courage to try

Acknowledgments

This book originated from the express request of several members of Courage for a book on the practice of chastity in a single life for people with a homosexual orientation. After considering the possibility of such a book, blending both psychological and spiritual insights, I decided that a discussion of the subject of chastity for all single people, along with clergy and religious, could be useful.

For a time I avoided reading or rereading a number of books on the single life and on celibacy which had been well received. I did not want unconsciously to use other writers' ideas. Yet their works are so valuable that I did not wish to leave them out. For this reason I have added a select, annotated bibliography which may be helpful.

Several people have assisted with this book at various stages. I wish to thank in particular Dr. Susan A. Muto of the Institute of Formative Spirituality at Duquesne University who so generously provided the introduction and suggestions. Like the founder of that institute, Father Adrian Van Kaam, she has provided many insights into the Christian life in our times. I am very grateful to Father John Harvey, O.S.F.S., founder of Courage, for his many suggestions. My profound indebtedness to St. Augustine, that holy and much misrepresented psychologist, is obvious on every page. I thank all whom I have been privileged to counsel in their struggles to be chaste and especially those who have allowed me to use anecdotes from their lives to illustrate parts of this book.

I wish to express my gratitude to all who worked on this book, especially Dr. John Farina of Paulist Press for his insights, Charles Pendergast for his invaluable assistance in editing, and to Father Glenn Sudano, O.F.M. Cap., for his suggestions and for checking the manuscript, and to Karin Samuel and Elaine Barone for typing. My thanks go also to Father William Smith of St. Joseph's Seminary, Dunwoodie, for his helpful comments.

Finally I am grateful to be guided by the Holy Catholic Church and her teachings. The Church is a guide in troubled waters. She gives us the sacramental help of Christ, without whom healthy chaste celibacy is impossible. She calls down upon us the Holy Spirit who always gives us the courage to be what we ought to be.

Benedict J. Groeschel
Larchmont, New York
Feast of the Assumption of Our Lady, 1984

Introduction
by Dr. Susan Annette Muto

The mystery of singleness is manifested in the unique beauty of each person, and, in a special way, in the lifestyle of the man or woman who happens to be single, either by choice or by circumstance. My book *Celebrating the Single Life* (Doubleday, 1982) was an attempt, based on personal experience, to highlight the realistic limits and joyful possibilities of being a celibate in the world. Its chief concern was to draw forth inner and outer obstacles to single living and to suggest conditions that facilitate delighting in, rather than decrying, one's single state.

While *Celebrating the Single Life* provided overall guidelines for a spirituality for single persons in today's world, this book by Father Groeschel dwells on one factor characteristic of a celibate life, namely, chaste loving. It is immensely refreshing to find the author describing the single person again and again as warm, tender, compassionate, friendly, dedicated, joyful. He cautions against a gloomy, self-pitying approach to singleness that may sadly seek relief in uncommitted, immoral relationships. Rightly, he sees the life of chastity as dynamic, self-donating, courageous.

His observation, supported by current research, posits that the so-called "sexual revolution" is on the wane, and that people are once again seeking transcendent values along with the commitments to chaste singleness and marital fidelity that accompany them. This book is meant to encourage those on the way to committed

1

singleness and to confirm those who have opted for this form of discipleship in response to God's grace.

It is a fact of our time that for some people preoccupation with sexuality outweighs concern for spirituality. Their "god" becomes personal gratification. They brag about conquests in the fashion of a Don Juan. But this "one-night-stand" mentality ultimately proves demeaning. Not only does one risk the permanent loss of self-respect; one may also end up totally alone, without friends, without family ties, and, worst of all, without God.

To drive this point home, Father Groeschel surfaces throughout his book the experience of St. Augustine. He shows how Augustine's bent toward vital pleasure severed from the Transcendent cast him into deep confusion, darkness of mind, and near-despair. It was only when this noble soul let go of his egocentric illusions and embraced Truth that he could experience peace of heart and pursue the Lord with the same vitality he had previously invested in empty pleasures.

It is important to remember, as the author does, that human sexuality is a gift of God. It permeates every dimension of our male/female being. Chaste living does not mean the repression of sexuality but the rechanneling of these energies, first of all in the pursuit of God with a passion characteristic of saints, and secondly in service of others in a way that is progressively freed from selfish interests.

One can only understand, and then never totally, the practice of voluntary abstinence from genital expressions of sexuality in the context of a contemplative longing to let God be the sole object of one's desire. This grace, as Father Groeschel points out, has to be fully appraised, perhaps with the help of a spiritual director, before, during and after making a commitment to the celibate life. Such a commitment, faithfully lived, requires courage. Indeed, this book is aptly titled *The Courage To Be Chaste*.

The word "courage" is related to the French word "coeur," which means "heart." What the author is trying to do in this book is to form the heart of the person called to the life of chastity. He takes as one of the keynotes of this vocation the Beatitude which states: "Blessed are the pure in heart, for they shall see God."

Another related book of mine, *Blessings That Make Us Be* (Crossroad, 1982) observes, in keeping with Father Groeschel's own thinking, that in this Beatitude Jesus blesses those whose hearts have been purified of self-love, so much so that they are able to radiate the love of God to others. This appears to be a fitting description of the kind of single person celebrated in this book. Because others see God in such disciples, Jesus promised them that they shall behold the Father. When the heart of the single person is one with the heart of Christ, he or she may readily glimpse God in this life and point the way to an eternal seeing of Him in the hereafter.

Those blessed with single-hearted love will gradually come to see their bodies not as objects separated from their spirit, to be used or abused at will, but as beautiful organisms serving the incarnation of gifts and talents, of aspirations and inspirations. They let go of the illusion of exalted, autonomous control and grow in the awareness of themselves as servants of a loving Mystery that calls each unique person to a life of union and communion.

Singleness of heart thus fosters the kind of seeing that enables us to view life and world against the horizon of the Transcendent. The pure of heart do not try to short-circuit this process of discipleship and cross-bearing. They know that it is only against the background of suffering and sacrifice that their Easter joy can be complete. Chaste living enables them to see more clearly the More Than in the midst of the ordinary, the Sacred in the secular, the Timeless in the timely.

When our hearts are singly oriented to these transcendent meanings, we may find that gradually, over a lifetime, God's love begins to suffuse our entire being, to direct our whole life. The goal of this life, as the author so frequently implies, is harmony. It is a style of living centered in Christ, in the Absolute Beauty, who is the source of goodness and the goal of our longing.

Such purity can never be our own accomplishment. It is the work of the Lord in us, the gift of His grace. The fruits of this commitment, courageously lived, will show up in such dispositions as joy, patience, mercy, gentleness, peace, trustworthiness, self-control, compassion and service. In the common life of home or business, in the drabness of passing days, in the moments of joy or sorrow, we are called to see the Lord as we are seen by Him. To be pure of heart is to see His Face where others may see only frustration, loneliness, disharmony, alienation. By contrast, Jesus saw the Face of the Father in all of creation. This seeing is His gift to the single-hearted. My wish is that those who read this book will come to know in a new way that the God who loved us first is one with us and that in our intention to be chaste, as well as in our actual living of this commitment, we are well on the way to becoming one with Him.

Preface

This book is meant to be a practical guide for those Christians attempting to lead a chaste single life. It is written not only for clergy and religious who have assumed the obligation of celibacy, but also for the single people who do not intend or expect to marry. Although the reasons for deciding to avoid all directly sought sexual intimacy may vary from person to person, the challenges of living a well-balanced and satisfying life without direct genital expression are essentially the same for all.

I have purposely directed this book to all who intend to remain unmarried, whether they are religious, single, widowed, or divorced, or have a homosexual orientation or other sexual conflict; in a word, to all who have accepted the Gospel call to chastity as the resolution of their sexual needs. I have tried to keep in mind those who wanted to marry but never had the opportunity, as well as those who, for reasons of their own, rejected the opportunity when it came along. Only the married and the premarried, that is, those who expect to marry in the foreseeable future and are preparing for marriage, are not taken into account here. They need a book of their own which could probably be written best by someone committed to chastity in the married life.

Several titles for this book suggest themselves, including "Everything You Ever Wanted To Know About Chastity But Were Afraid To Ask" and (my favorite) "Chastity with Pizzaz." I prefer the latter because I have enjoyed the fruits of chastity in my own life (although I did not always relish its challenges). A Christian single life has brought me a host of friends, including dozens of children with troubled backgrounds who have no one to call "father" but me.

My life as a priest committed to chastity has been far from limiting; on the contrary, it has opened up engaging relationships and experiences which, at times, seemed to distract me from my primary goal which is to seek God. Rather than removing me from family life, chastity has given me several families of contrasting social and economic situations, belonging to different religions, races and cultures.

Chastity has enabled me to help people for whom sexuality had become a burden, a trap, a curse, or, in the case of those caught in prostitution, a form of slavery. Such assistance has been possible because those in difficulty were able to trust someone vowed to a life of celibacy.

Most important, chastity has summoned me at the beginning and end of each day to continue the journey to God. Any good life is a road to God and the best road is the one that He has chosen for the individual. But celibate chastity is a special help. The single man or woman striving to lead a chaste life reaches out to God with empty arms, alone with the Alone. Historically, the single person has always had many companions, including numerous saints who have followed the call of Christ alone. Even the person in a religious community knows that a celibate life is not, and cannot be, a substitute for a living spouse. Celibacy has its own challenges and blessings. Christian celibates need to make no apologies, but they may profit by some suggestions and encouragement.

This book is meant to encourage chaste, unmarried persons who are trying to be integrated followers of Christ. Chastity is best considered a goal rather than a static condition. Each day brings new challenges, new trials, and, for some, new failures. Perhaps only great saints and mystics are perfectly chaste, in the sense that they have all their emotions, desires and impulses under complete control. For the rest of us it is a struggle, a fight with either partial failure or total defeat.

To be chaste is a daily adventure in growth and discovery and, as with any adventure, there are many dangers and close calls. Getting wounded is a real possibility that has to be coped with before, during and after a fall. For this reason courage is necessary if one is to be chaste. Courage is a moral virtue and a gift of the Holy Spirit. To be chaste—whether as a married or single person—we need both.

I gratefully give credit to those who have provided me with the key word in the title of this book, "Courage." A group of men and women united by a decision to lead a chaste Christian life despite homosexual tendencies has chosen this word to designate their movement. Their faith and courage, as well as their reliance on the Holy Spirit and His gift of courage, first prompted the writing of this book.

I have borrowed liberally from the writings of St. Augustine. No Christian writer has left a more honest account of his struggles for chastity. The quotations from *The Confessions* are particularly helpful for meditation. They convey the special vitality of the translator, Frank Sheed. I was privileged to discuss Augustine's attitudes on chastity with this great Catholic apologist, who helped me to see that the "holy psychologist" had much to say to the struggling Christians of our own time.

Part 1

The Challenge of a Chaste Life

1

Living a Chaste Single Life in Today's World

A few years ago a young religious sister shared the following experience. She was enrolled at a state university in a course entitled "Human Sexuality." She attended class anonymously and was unrecognized as a sister. For reasons unknown (and probably unknowable), the students were required to share with the class the wildest sexual encounter they had experienced. Sister resolved to stand her ground and admit the awful truth—she had never had a sexual encounter.

As this exhibitionist's round-robin made its way to her, she disclosed her dreadful secret. The students thought they had been prepared for everything, but not for this! Chastity was just too far out. Between their gasps of incomprehension and guffaws of unbelief, she managed to explain that she was a religious sister. The response of the group completely reversed. Her classmates were delighted, awe-struck and deeply moved. They all agreed that she should stay right where she was and not have an encounter. Even the most jaded were impressed to know that someone, somewhere, had managed to preserve her humanity and yet be chaste for the Kingdom of God.

While this incident reveals the remarkable attraction for the ideal of chastity among those who are culturally conditioned to reject it, nevertheless, the young person, whether married or single, who attempts to lead a chaste Christian life is going to meet a withering amount of opposition. In thirty years, motion pictures and other forms of entertainment have gone from the avoidance of sexuality to the explicit exploitation of lust. Most Christian denominations which had clearly defined codes of sexual mores have adopted libertarian attitudes that history is likely to judge as severely as it judges the seamy side of the Italian Renaissance or the French Enlightenment.

A Working Definition of Chastity

Single Christians, whether young or old, must live in opposition to the strong tide of contemporary decadence. I do not intend to confuse the issue for them by entering the debate over the meaning of chastity. There are aspects of this theological discussion which interest me, but perhaps only because they would give me dangerous opportunities to use sarcasm and irony in uncharitable ways. I will rely on the traditional Christian meaning of chastity accepted by an army of spiritual and moral writers (many of them canonized saints) up to the present time. This definition has been reiterated by Pope John Paul II and is clearly summarized in the pastoral reflection on morality of the American Catholic bishops, "To Live in Christ Jesus,"[1] a sadly forgotten but powerful document. It has been restated more recently in unambiguous terms by the Sacred Congregation for Catholic Education.[2]

I use the terms chaste celibacy and chaste single life to mean the avoidance of all voluntary genital and pregenital sexual behavior. They also imply a decision to avoid personal relationships of human affection which are likely to be genitally expressed. This is an obligation for the vowed celibate and for the person who cannot validly enter marriage.

A Christian who decides to remain single has, in fact, opted for the same expression of chastity as that chosen by the vowed celibate.

---

1. National Conference of Catholic Bishops, Washington D.C.: U.S. Catholic Conference, 1976.

2. Educational Guidance in Human Love, Nov. 1, 1983. Available from St. Paul Editions, 50 St. Paul's Ave., Boston, Ma. 02130.

Chastity for all Christians means avoiding sexual satisfaction from auto-eroticism or from deviant behavior. It does *not* mean isolation, rejection of human love and friendship, or refraining from certain non-genital behavior related to the expression of one's sexuality. Chastity implies an heroic effort at times to confront the dark and self-centered aspects of one's inner being.

If you are not generally in agreement with the above definition, this book is not for you. If, on the other hand, you live by or would like to live by these Christian values, which are rooted in the Scriptures and tradition of your faith, you may find this book helpful.

Everyone knows that Christian marriage calls couples to a very challenging form of chastity. There are many similarities between the struggles of married and single believers. In this book we are limiting ourselves to a consideration of those who intend to remain unmarried. At times we may apply the word *chastity* to the single state but there is no implication that it is reserved to that state.

Obstacles to a Chaste Life

Twice in the past decade writers of satire in the *New York Times* Book Review have listed and reviewed imaginary books on chastity, written by imaginary authors, on one occasion by a mythical nun. On both occasions the book was a defense of or guide to celibate chastity. These imaginary titles were listed among other books entitled "Aboriginal Gourmet Cooking" and "How To Build Your Own Space Craft."

It was all very funny in a sick way, but it also indicated the lack of sensitivity of our times. The authors of these satires were civilized men who, I am sure, never meant to be offensive. They should have realized, however, that a high proportion of religious read their book reviews. No doubt their grandmothers taught them, as mine taught me, that it is in poor taste to make fun of other people's religious practices. Perhaps it never occurred to these and other educated scorners of chastity that there are a fair number of people trying to lead the life that they had chosen to mock.

Mockers are simply part of a situation (I hesitate to call it a culture) that accepts misfortune as the only legitimate excuse for leading a celibate life. While those who belittle chastity might admire St. Francis or Mother Teresa, they never come to grips with religious chastity as an integral part of the dynamics and life adjustment of such people. They might admire Gandhi, but they ignore his struggle to observe celibate religious chastity while his wife was still living and very dear to him. A celibate person without the mystique of Gandhi or St. Francis is likely to win only their scorn.

Misunderstanding and Mockery

The negative reactions that the celibate single person encounters are not always mocking; they range from pity to disbelief. In the case of a person who is young and not in a religious community, relatives and friends decide that there must be something psychologically wrong. Even religious and clerics of marriageable age may have a relative or friend suggest that it might be time "to get out and live a normal married life." Young people intending to try a religious vocation experience various attitudes that range from compassion to ridicule. The one conclusion we can reach from all of this is that voluntary chastity is not a vocation for the faint-hearted.

Anyone who is determined as a result of a religious conversion to be chaste after a life of sexual indulgence, either heterosexual or homosexual, will find out where friendship has its roots. Deliberate attempts will be made to lure the newly converted back to the fleshpots. St. Augustine describes how he attempted to entice one of his boon companions from the Christian life when he was seventeen, and how terrible he felt when the young man died. This revealed to Augustine that he himself had not been a true friend.[3]

3. Cf. *The Confessions.* IV.iv., trans. F. J. Sheed, New York: Sheed & Ward, 1978, pp. 48-49.

What motivates so many to oppose celibate chastity? It may be a human concern that someone not miss an engaging part of life. I think of the sweet old Jewish lady who told her husband to take me for a walk "and explain things" when she found out I was going off to the monastery as a teenager. Or it may be the reaction of those who are conflicted themselves; they feel a call to chastity which they cannot or will not accept. Or it may be the old insane American fallacy that causes resentment toward anyone who disagrees with prevailing values because, the theory goes, if we all agree, we must be right. Or, God forbid, it may even be a very base impulse from the dark part of the human psyche which seeks to destroy that which is beautiful in another person.

I recall working with a man who was vowed to religious chastity. A woman friend literally pursued him. Her conscious motivation, I suspect, was to bring some love into what she perceived as his loveless life. He actually relinquished his calling and left in order to marry her. Incredibly, she refused to see him at all after he was released from his vows. While I do not accuse this young woman of malicious intent, I suspect that she was subconsciously motivated by a desire to destroy something she did not possess.

This strange case forcefully brought home to me what I have read in the works of great psychologists, namely, that much sexual motivation is unconscious and, consequently, can be dangerous and self-destructive. Anyone who chooses to make the struggle for celibate chastity must look beyond simple sexual need and pleasure to discover the real motivations. Pleasure or its deliberate renunciation is rarely an adequate explanation of either sexual indulgence or chastity.

Going beyond the superficial hedonism of everyday life, Dag Hammarskjöld, a single man, reveals in his diary, *Markings*, his struggle to be chaste and his religious motivation. He has this to say about the dark side of human nature:

> *We can reach the point where* it becomes possible for us to recognize and understand Original Sin, that dark counter-

center of evil in our nature—that is to say, though it *is* not our nature, it is *of* it—that something within us which rejoices when disaster befalls the very cause we are trying to serve, or misfortune overtakes even those whom we love.

Life in God is not an escape from this, but the way to gain full insight concerning it.

It is when we stand in the righteous all-seeing light of love that we can dare to look at, admit, and *consciously* suffer under this something in us which wills disaster, misfortune, defeat to everything outside the sphere of our narrowest self-interest. So a living relation to God is the necessary precondition for the self-knowledge which enables us to follow a straight path, and so be victorious over ourselves, forgiven by ourselves.[4]

The Suspicion of Pathology

There are more subtle objections to chastity than those alluded to so far. Perhaps the most obvious is the belief that chastity is an impossible ideal. Contemporary psychology, especially in its "pop" forms, has created the illusion that sexual abstinence is impossible, except in the case of severe pathology.

There is no doubt that a human life without sexuality is impossible. Defining chastity as a life without sexuality is a denial of human nature. Indeed, some Catholics who ridicule chastity are, in fact, reacting to that past definition of chastity. If, however, we define chastity as a life without voluntary genital behavior, we express a very different reality. Many people live such lives without any symptoms of serious pathology.

The inaccuracies of pop psychology and its need to cater to a large audience explain why popular writers rarely make a distinction in favor of sane celibacy. More thoughtful psychologists like Erik Erikson made such a distinction long ago. In his classic work *Childhood and Society* written in 1950, Erikson, while discussing generativity as the form of maturity, wrote:

4. *Markings*. New York: Alfred A. Knopf, 1966, pp. 127-128.

Where philosophical and spiritual tradition suggests the renunciation of the right to procreation or to produce, such
(persons) early turn to "ultimate concerns" whenever in-
stituted into monastic movements; (this tradition) strives to
settle at the same time the relationship to the care for the
creatures of this world and to the Charity which is felt to
transcend it.[5]

Although many celibate single people have made significant
contributions to human welfare while leading creative and happy
lives, the prejudice remains that anyone whose life is without
genital sexuality is either ill-informed or psychologically crippled.
There is no doubt that in the normative human life, the mature
individual exchanges love and affection faithfully with a partner of
the other sex and shares most aspects of life, especially the great
task of raising the next generation. Genital sexuality is an element
in the lives of most human beings and surely it was meant to be so.
But as Erikson has pointed out, one can direct much energy to the
care of other people's children and to the search for God as the
first object of desire. This must be the goal of the single Christian
attempting to live the Gospel.

It is important to remember that some people pursuing such non-
religious goals as science or creative art have renounced marriage
and, apparently, genital sexuality. While we are not concerned
here with these people, they do provide another interesting
example of persons being celibate and creative at the same time.

Sexual Bombardment

The single person, and indeed any Christian who is committed to
chastity both before and during marriage, lives in a world of
continuous sexual bombardment from advertising, media and
entertainment. This undoubtedly makes a chaste life more
difficult. Some people handle this by selective withdrawal from
life, which is not the best way to adjust to the problem. It is far

---

5. *Childhood and Society.* New York: Norton (2nd edition), 1963, p. 268.

better to be on the offensive than on the defensive, to assert one's preferences firmly and let others know when something is personally offensive or distasteful.

Perhaps one of the most persistent and obviously invalid assumptions of our civilization is that sexual behavior brings happiness. The media trumpet the message, "Sex brings happiness." If this were true, we would indeed live in an earthly paradise, and the world would be "Happy Valley."

I suppose that half the people you meet on a bus, or in a shopping center, or even at church on Sunday have had some genital sexual experience during the preceding few days. It is the observation of an old celibate from way back that they are not all so very happy. If sex brought happiness, the world would shine like the sun, at least half the time. Celibates need not try to convince themselves that chaste celibacy is the road to earthly bliss, but on the other hand they need not feel deprived of the key to happiness. If there is a single key to contentment, it cannot be sexual experience.

Loneliness

Loneliness—the painful awareness of the need for companionship and support—is probably the greatest obstacle to chastity in the single life. Obviously, the single person has to value aloneness, the state of being on one's own. He or she must also have learned to overcome loneliness, that is, aloneness when it becomes a burden.

Yet the better things of life are often organized for couples—even parish and religious activities. Parties, entertainment, time off and vacations often accentuate loneliness for the single. We will consider later how a single person must energetically organize his or her life, so that loneliness does not become an occasion for unwanted sexual desire or even sexual compulsion.

The Stigma of Being Single

We have already seen that poorly applied pop psychology may leave the single person feeling like a cripple. This adds to the special burden of those who are unmarried by reason of apparent misfortune, or against their own choice. This group usually does not include clergy and religious, although I have noted this sentiment among religious who wish they could live their lives again.

No doubt many single people would prefer to have married, but the opportunity never came their way or, if it did, it did not seem appropriate for them. Others are widowed or divorced and not inclined to marry again. In the case of the divorced, remarriage may not be possible because of moral principles and Church teaching. Other single people do not consider marriage an option for them because they recognize their lack of psycho-sexual development, or because they realize their strong homosexual inclinations. Certain people suffer very quietly with deviant sexual desires and do not want to jeopardize another person's happiness with their problem. Many others just like to be independent.

Some years ago I met an attractive young woman who was very active in the charismatic renewal. We shall call her Maryanne. She has a deep and well-informed commitment to the spiritual life. Maryanne had accepted peacefully, even joyfully, the knowledge that she would have to lead a chaste single life. Far from being reluctant about her decision, she embraced the chaste Christian life gratefully.

For some years before her conversion to an intense Christian life, Maryanne had been actively involved in a series of homosexual relationships. She had lived on the quiet, respectable edge of "the gay scene." No one meeting this young woman now would think of her as unhappy or frustrated. Determination, a positive self-image replete with self-acceptance and a real concern for others emanate from her personality. This is no mask. Maryanne proves to many that a chaste life can be a fulfilling, creative and joyful experience.

The Vocation of the Chaste Disciple

Whatever their original motives, many single people we have been speaking of are sincere Christians and want to make their lives

chaste. In the past they may have taken the edge off temptation by
indulging in auto-eroticism, or by "affairs" with no notion of
permanent commitment, or by other unsatisfactory and morally
conflicted behavior. Choosing to be celibate will bring them not
only peace with God but also a sense of integrity and nobility of
life. It will also teach (as nothing else can) a great reliance on the
grace of Christ and the need to be saved from themselves. A
single life led unwillingly and marred by unchaste behavior is
indeed a pitiful thing. A life of chastity led with prayerful love of
God and neighbor is a most worthy form of discipleship, regardless
of the personal factors that prompted the individual to be single.

There is an obvious difference between the life of a married
Christian and a chaste single life. A marriage can become a noble
Christian discipleship, even if it did not begin with a mature
decision. Spouses can be converted together and grow together in
Christ. Sexuality which may be little more than an expression of
need or dependency can grow to be the profound expression of the
sacramental presence of Christ in a relationship of human love.
Even if the couple does not arrive at these lofty heights, their
relationship may be a genuine struggle for discipleship with joys
and sorrows, failures and successes experienced together.
Repentance shared by a couple can be a beautiful experience.

In the same way, when opting for the single life, a person may not
have considered it a form of discipleship. I have met clergy and
religious who gave the vow of chastity little thought before they
took it; it was simply part of the price of admission to their
vocation. The single person, lay or religious, may suddenly find his
or her attempt at chastity threatened, or in ruins. This is an
opportunity for real conversion and commitment. But it takes
insight, self-knowledge, energetic planning, and a great reliance
on the grace of God to do anything as worthwhile and complex as
leading a well-balanced chaste life. In a word, a chaste life—like a
solid Christian marriage—calls for discipleship.

In writing this book I have drawn on the experience of many
people who are trying to lead chaste lives despite the obstacles

enumerated above; I have also drawn on my own experience with this struggle. For all Christians, married, single or religious, chastity is not simply a struggle with physical urges and drives. It is part of the greater effort to seek God above and through all things. Chastity is an aspect of purity of mind and heart, of thought and desire. Like every worthwhile thing in life, chastity is a struggle which has its rewards. They are summed up in the Beatitude, "How blessed are the pure of heart, for they shall see God."

2

Understanding Your Choice of a Celibate Life

If you expect to live a celibate life, and hope to do so chastely, it is essential to understand the reasons for making your choice. You must strive by intelligent insight to understand yourself, just as a married couple must come to understand each other, whether they do so with words, or attitudes expressed in gestures. As a single person with no spouse to share your most intimate feelings, you must rely on conscious ideas and clear thinking.

In this chapter I will try to interpret what seem to be the most common reasons for choosing a single life. Such motives as a religious vocation or previous failure at marriage may not pertain to you at all, and you may skip over them. But don't be too easy on yourself and assume that your motivation is simply a desire to be single. Life is more complicated than that.

The Religious Vocation

In the Western or Roman branch of the Catholic Church, celibacy with all the obligations of a chaste single life has been required of priests since the fourth century. Religious or monastic life for men and women has always required celibacy in all world religions. In most religions, including Catholicism, celibacy has been interpreted as sexual abstinence, or chastity. Until about thirty years ago, large numbers of men and women who felt called to the priesthood or religious life accepted this responsibility. If chastity was considered at all, it was usually confronted in a very personal way with such questions as: "Can I do it?" "Can I break off with Rosemary?" "Can I make it without Bill?"

In previous days of cultural denial of sexuality in the public media (remember the old romantic films where love stopped at the neck?), talks and conferences on chastity gave the impression that once the decision was made, that was it! You had only to watch for the reincarnation of some Jezebel and get lots of exercise, if you wanted to die safely with a perfect scorecard. Some of my young friends belonged to a society to promote chastity that was dedicated to St. Thomas Aquinas, known for his angelic purity. They received a diploma, showing St. Thomas being girdled by two hefty female angels (so it appeared), while a scarlet figure escaped down a long cloister. On the threshold lay a burning torch which, according to legend, the saint had used to chase away the lady of doubtful virtue whom his family had sent to seduce him. Nothing puritanical about the Aquinas clan.

I must confess now that I was piously envious of my friends whose efforts to be chaste were so well recognized, even though it was a secret society. It is worth noting that all these devotees of the angelic battle for purity lost the war, and I, without a diploma, went on to spend half my life working with poor souls who the world thought were women of doubtful virtue, none of whom ever so much as winked an eye at me. Just as well, because I did not have a fireplace in my office, and, consequently, no burning torch to make me feel safe.

The Church and many of her most committed children have paid a high price for a celibacy that was sincere, but poorly understood. The present-day struggle for celibacy by religious and clergy has been a star-crossed battle. Not only did the old puritanism leave people ill-prepared to understand their commitment to celibacy, but the new age of sexual expression dawned at the same time that selfism (as a value) became a strong element in popular psychology.

Selfism, an ineptly concocted psychological theory, holds that one must be neurotic not to activate all potentials and fulfill all desires. It has undermined religious commitment as well as many marriages and families with a philosophy of life completely at odds with the teaching of Jesus Christ in the Gospel.[1] Add to all of this the theological dislocation that frequently follows a successful ecumenical council, and the stage is set for a widespread loss of commitment to celibate religious life. From a practical point of view, sexuality has been the greatest focus of conflict in the post-conciliar period.

At this point, dear reader, you may be trying to understand your commitment to celibacy, or you may be thinking of making this commitment in the future. Despite all that has happened since the mid-1960s, a surprising number of young people, especially young men, continue to make this commitment in the face of an unsympathetic world.

If you are going to lead a chaste religious life, your primary motive should be to fulfill what you believe is the will of God for you. You are responding to a vocation, a call to be Christ's disciple in this challenging way. Even the most skeptical unbeliever who thinks you are making a big mistake will have to admit that you are trying to walk the straight way and enter the narrow gate. You need apologize to no one for following this call, since nearly half the recognized heroes and heroines of the human race have done so. You do need a profound sense of reliance on God and the realization that what you are attempting is impossible for human nature unaided by grace.

Not long ago it was in vogue among religious writers to stress the normality of the celibate vocation. I thought it a very odd use of the word normal, which literally means average. I wasn't completely surprised when many "normal" celibates gave it all up.

Religious celibacy is extraordinary in all dimensions. Its origin, purposes, witness and value are all beyond the ordinary superficial

---

1. Daniel Yankelovich, *New Rules*. New York: Random House, 1981. Cf. Part I for an excellent analysis of selfism.

notions on which everyday life is organized. It is an extraordinary call which God directs to otherwise ordinary men and women. That is what grace is all about; that is what the Gospel is about. That is what Christ means in this remarkable passage:

> The disciples said to him, "If that is how things are between husband and wife, it is not advisable to marry." But he replied, "It is not everyone who can accept what I have said, but only those to whom it is granted. There are eunuchs born that way from their mother's womb, there are eunuchs made so by men and there are eunuchs who have made themselves that way for the sake of the kingdom of heaven. Let anyone accept this who can" (Mt 19:10–12).

The Simply Single Person

The single person is one who never accepted, or never had, the opportunity to marry. Prejudice against the single in our society has been a constant theme, and to this day it affects all but the swinging singles of the "sophisticated" set, who are presumed not to be chaste anyway. If you are one of the singles outside the jet set, you had better come on strong. Don't be afraid to look at the reasons why you are single. They may be quite cogent and even noble. But usually the motives are more complex than they seem, so consider all the possibilities before deciding about yourself. Here are some of the most frequently given reasons.

The Right Person Never Came Along

This is the most common conscious reason people give for remaining single. It is a good reason, as anyone who married the wrong person will tell you. In our society, most marriages are built on psychological complementarity, rather than on economic need, and they require a good deal of mutual sharing along with affection and caring. Even affection, sexually expressed or not, is often not enough to make a marriage go smoothly. For the Christian there must be the belief that Providence has directed the choice of a spouse. Some people must accept that, in the Providence of God,

they have been called to a single life. Worse things could happen!
Think of the lady who married the vampire!

Behind the statement that the right person never came along may
lie many unrecognized factors. A person may indeed have been too
particular, or unprepared to share life in all the complexities of
marriage. There may have been a genuine fear of sexuality, of the
unknown and the dangerous. There may have been a general
failure to make friends outside one's own family. These are not the
best reasons to opt for the single life, because they indicate
limitations or shortcomings on the part of the individual.

If you suspect that some of these reasons were part of your choice
to be single, you must accept this and deal with it creatively.
Certainly many married people discover that they entered a
marriage for motives which were not the best. How many women
say that they married "to get out of the house"? And how many
men admit that they simply needed someone to care for them? But
just as a couple can pick up the pieces and do better by improving
their motives and expectations of marriage, so can a single person.
Certainly the decision to lead a chaste, productive and generous
life is the beginning of such a new identity for the single.

A word should be said about the person who developed fairly high
spiritual goals early in life. In our society, where sex is presented
as a form of recreation rather than as a sign of commitment in
marriage, a spiritually motivated single person may find it a
heartbreaking and almost impossible task to look for an appropriate
spouse. Many fine young women have complained to me about
this difficulty. They are afraid to date because they do not wish to
be morally compromised. They hesitate to think about religious
life because so many communities appear unstable and unsure of
their own identity; thus, the prospect of a reluctantly accepted
single life stands threateningly before them.

A good question for someone in this position is: Am I looking for a
degree of spiritual maturity and perfection in another that I have
not achieved myself? A potential spouse may still be searching for

solid spiritual values. As I pointed out in my book *Spiritual Passages*, the first phase of the spiritual journey is often filled with conflicts and failure.[2] Perhaps a person with spiritual values wishes sincerely, but unrealistically, to marry a guru. That's very unrealistic because gurus usually don't get married.

The Person With Other Things To Do

Those who analyze motives of the single as a pastime jump on those who claim that they had other things to do, but the fact is that in many lives this may be true. In many families a person remains single to take care of parents or some other family member. Some single people have chosen to pursue a career, and marriage is out of the question during the long training period. That is more often the case with women than with men. Since there are more women than men, there will be more unmarried women who will care for their parents or enter a career. In addition, many people in our society are considering single life as a viable option, which is being recognized in secular psychological circles.

Having chosen to be single, the individual ought to review the unrecognized motives I mentioned in the last section. This is particularly true if one is dissatisfied with and depressed about being single. (The old refrain, "If I had it to do all over again," is not the exclusive property of the married or religious.) Frequently a person who remains single for personal reasons will experience some of the sexual difficulties resulting from frustration. We will discuss these in Chapter 6.

The attempt to live a chaste single life is a specific form of discipleship. The awareness of discipleship is a great help to a person because it gives a purpose and goal to the price of singleness. One's self-respect and, consequently, one's ability to be a blessing to others will be greatly enhanced by a firm commitment to discipleship. A clear intellectual understanding of unconscious motivation will serve to strengthen that commitment.

---

2. New York: Crossroad, 1983.

Single People Who Have Been Married

The Widowed

Many widowed people choose to remain single. This decision may
stem from a deeply felt loyalty to the deceased spouse or from a
recognition that another marriage may be too complicated and
demanding. Chastity is often a problem for such people because
sexual activity had become part of the rhythm of life.

Many recently widowed people, however, experience their
greatest religious fervor at this time of life. Faith in eternal life and
prayer are their principal support. Their love and appreciation of
Christ as Savior are constantly growing, and they become more
eager to follow the Gospel teachings. But grief, loneliness, and
alienation from couples who had been their friends leave them
more vulnerable to sexual impulses than they had ever been. Thus
there is a serious conflict for the widow or widower to which others
are often insensitive.

Again I suggest that they look at underlying motives for remaining
unmarried. If they accept these motives they must begin to live a
productive and balanced single life. Although being single is
unfamiliar to them, they have to learn to be on their own and like
it. If they don't like it, they should certainly entertain the
possibility of remarriage.

If you are a widow or widower who intends to remain unmarried,
don't sit around like a cup without a saucer. The following chapters
will make some valuable suggestions on how to lead an engaging
life which will make it easier to avoid unwanted sexual behavior,
especially auto-eroticism. A devout, peaceful and chaste life as a
widow or widower may transform someone who feels like a leftover
in life to a real Christian whose experience and compassion permit
a generosity to others which they never before dreamed of. It can
mean the difference between just growing old and growing to be a

significant and balanced parent figure or friend for many needy people.

The Divorced and the Annulled

Among the single are a growing number of people who have gone through the painful experience of the end of marriage. Even if they have an ecclesiastical annulment, many of these people do not wish to marry again. As a group of women told me whom I met at a meeting of Separated and Divorced Catholics, "We've had it!"

The transition to a single life, especially when one has children, is not easy. The divorced encounter many of the same difficulties as a young widow or widower, but they lack some of the social respectability, even though they may have had the best and most honorable motives. I heartily agree that more understanding of the divorced is needed in the Church.

If you are divorced and wish to lead a chaste, unmarried life, you ought to concentrate on your potentials rather than on the hardship of being divorced. Like all suffering, the process of divorce can mature a person. You are probably much more independent and self-reliant now than you used to be. You may have deepened your spiritual life out of necessity, as you went through the painful decision, separation and divorce proceedings. Perhaps you have had an enforced experience of sexual abstinence; if you are reading this book, then you have learned to live with this deprivation.

I suggest you turn what was a disaster into a positive vocation. We all know people who have grown immeasurably as the result of a paralyzing accident or other personal catastrophe. I know many people in Alcoholics Anonymous who are far better Christians than they would have been had they not experienced the horror of alcoholism. A marriage that ends in divorce is a tragedy, but tragedy can lead to growth and discipleship. Sooner or later we are going to get a patron saint for the divorced. Then the spiritual possibilities of the chaste celibate life-style in this situation will be formally recognized. In the meantime, if you are divorced, give it a try. You might even become the patron saint.

The Person Who Is Single out of Fear

Most people are afraid of sexuality in some way because it is such a powerful force. It can sometimes lead a person to destructive, even suicidal behavior. Most overcome this fear enough to marry, and they are able to cope with sexuality in this least threatening way.

Many men and women, however, are afraid of intimacy in general, and of sexual intimacy in particular. They may have grown up in environments which were overprotected, or, on the contrary, in which sexual indulgence was an obvious cause of discord and suffering. Sometimes a very frightening sexual experience as a child, especially with an adult, is likely to cause permanent fear of sexual intimacy. Individuals so traumatized may decide they cannot cope with all the demands of intimacy which a happy marriage requires.

If you have remained single out of fear, you may be young enough to consider in-depth counseling or psychotherapy to determine whether you can decide to marry or remain single with more freedom. It is best to choose a life-style with the greatest inner freedom possible. It may be too late to try such a project, however, and by now you may feel comfortable in a single life.

The problem is that those who are single out of fear often find that their sexual desires drive them to behavior that is morally unacceptable and personally humiliating. Subtle and disguised forms of sexual satisfaction may mar their lives. Attraction to unsavory forms of entertainment, indulgence of voyeuristic impulses, and promiscuous behavior may be the result of conflicted acceptance of a single life. A single life accepted out of fear is by no means necessarily a chaste life.

If you feel that you are single out of fear, this book may be a great help to you. It may open up the possibility of a genuine decision: a conscious, deliberate choice for a chaste single life. By following the Gospel and leading a chaste life you may experience a profound inner healing and come to a new sense of your Christian dignity. Self-pity and self-indulgence are often partners in keeping a person from a mature Christian life. If you are caught in the web of these two undesirable attitudes, the struggle to lead a chaste life may open up a whole new life for you.

The Single Homosexually Oriented Person

Only now are we becoming aware of the very large number of people in our world who struggle with some aspect of what is called "homosexuality." This complex psychological phenomenon which causes a person to be sexually attracted to members of his or her own sex must be discussed in some detail. We will present a more detailed analysis of chastity and the homosexually oriented person in Chapter 3; at present we will confine our discussion to homosexual tendencies as a motive for choosing the single life.

Many persons who think of themselves, rightly or wrongly, (and I believe often wrongly) as "homosexuals" have chosen to be single. Perhaps they are totally unattracted to marriage, or, if they have some attraction to it, they are unwilling to risk subjecting another person to the sorrow of a broken marriage. Some fantasize about entering a lasting, exclusive homosexual union, but such relationships are rare indeed.

My own clinical work with a fairly large number of homosexually oriented adults leads me to believe that many, if not most, homosexuals end up leading a single life with some casual sexual involvement or sexual friendship. Such a position keeps alive the illusion that the right partner is going to come along. Others simply withdraw from the homosexual scene and lead quiet lives with little sexual involvement. The turbulence of homosexual relationships, the danger of serious or fatal illness, and the fear of being exposed all motivate people to withdraw after the ardor of youth is over. Some, convinced that the traditional teaching of the Church is correct on the moral unacceptability of genital homosexual acts, try to lead chaste single lives, often with difficulty.

If you believe that homosexual tendencies make marriage impossible, you have two choices: lead a chaste celibate life, or one plagued by unwanted homosexual genital behavior. The teaching of Catholic tradition, reiterated clearly by the highest pastoral authority of the Church in our own time, calls the homosexual person to a chaste life.[3] You may find teachers, clerical and lay, who will tell you something different, but they cannot deny the Catholic tradition necessitating chastity in such cases.

If you would like to try to be chaste, or if you have already been leading a chaste life, this book is meant to help you. To be chaste while enduring homosexual tendencies is not easy, but it is by no means impossible, even if you have engaged in homosexual activity in the past. I have seen this struggle become an invitation to profound spiritual growth and a very holy life. I suspect there are even a number of canonized saints who have found a road to great holiness in this struggle.

The slaves of pleasure, be it related to sexuality or to some other compulsion, all sit in the same galley, although chained to different oars. And the free men and women of the Spirit all walk on the same road of holiness, even though they may have been drawn there through different experiences by the grace of the Holy Spirit.

The Single Who Struggle with Sexual Deviation

In my work as a priest and psychologist, I have met a number of persons who are single because they have experienced deviant sexual tendencies. Many psychologists and psychiatrists feel that

---

3. Cf. Pope John Paul II, Statement to American Bishops in Chicago, October 5, 1979.

these deviations, like homosexual tendencies, represent an arrested sexual development and fixation, or hangup, at an early stage of psychosexual development. They are unquestionably painful pathologies which can exist in the life of an otherwise productive and relatively well-adjusted individual.

The range of these pathologies is very large and some are not even popularly recognized as pathologies. For instance, a driven need to be heterosexually promiscuous is certainly a sexual deviation, although at present the amorality of the media may make a hero out of a sexual addict.

Such deviations as sado-masochistic tendencies are alarming to an individual, even if they are not acted out. Others, like exhibitionism or transvestism, are deeply embarrassing. Still others have serious legal consequences, for example, pedophilia, an attraction for children. Such deviations as fetishism (a compulsion to attach sexual significance to neutral objects) and voyeurism are simply a nuisance. There are too many other deviations to enumerate, but what we say here will apply to a person who suffers from any of them.

Many otherwise adjusted people suffer from one of these problems, and either have not had the opportunity for therapy or have found it unhelpful. The person with a deviation (a word which simply means "off the main track") may marry and keep the problem a secret from his or her spouse. However, it is likely that the person may choose to remain single. This decision, like the decision to remain single out of fear, may leave the individual with unfulfilled sexual needs and lead to many frustrations and humiliations. The single life will then become a curse, and the deviation may take hold and mar the person's entire life.

In this case, the call to a chaste single life may actually be a tremendous relief. It may offer a way out of a nightmare. Nevertheless, such a person always needs the help of an informed confessor or spiritual director, and may be well advised to try therapy again in the new life-situation where there is the positive goal of a life that is chaste and productive. The individual should not feel responsible for deviant tendencies which arise from circumstances in early life. It is important to stress this, for they can make a person feel like an outcast from God and man. The chastity which Christ offers to those who will follow His way may be the only real way out of a difficult situation. He says to all, "Come to Me, all you who are heavily burdened" (Mt 11:28).

The Right To Be Single and Happy

No one has to apologize for being single. Like every human situation apart from a life of sin, singleness can be a call to discipleship. If you find yourself apologizing for being single, that is your problem and no one else's.

Many single people are their own worst enemies. They choose to live in such a way that they are bound to feel miserable and alienated. Unfulfilled sexual needs that are toyed with and sometimes furtively satisfied become a great frustration and a lonely passion.

But there is a better way. "Happy are they who walk according to the law of the Lord" (Ps 119:1). Happy, or blessed, means just that—at peace, contented, even in the midst of difficulty. In these unhappy and unbelieving times, the single Christian, lay or religious, should be a witness to the peace that the world cannot give. One cannot give this witness simply by avoiding forbidden behavior. This witness, as we shall see, is a whole way of life.

3

Sexuality in a
Chaste Single Life

A number of psychotherapists have pointed out in recent years
that a common factor in the lives of those with serious sexual
problems is unrealism, a deeply rooted unwillingness to accept
reality. The acceptance, or affirmation, of reality is the starting
point for any struggle with oneself, and, according to Van Kaam,
the beginning of the therapeutic change.[1]

Anyone with serious sexual problems is always waiting
unrealistically for Queen Guenivere or Sir Galahad, for the perfect
lady or the white knight to come along. Paradoxically, one of the
most dangerous forms of this unrealism is to think that one can live
without sexuality. This is the old heresy of manicheism or
albigensianism which long ago led to terrible sexual excesses on
the part of those who sought to be absolutely pure. These
misguided heretics are a reminder that one of the most dangerous
sexual unrealisms is the pretense that humans can be angels.

Accepting and living with the reality that God made us bodily
creatures does not mean that we must voluntarily indulge in sexual
pleasure. It does mean recognizing that our sexuality will often be
felt and experienced in many ways. Because sexual expression in
its highest form is linked with tender emotions and the need for

---

1. Adrian Van Kaam, *The Art of Existential Counseling*. Denville, N.J.:
Dimension Books,1966, Chapter III.

intimacy, the person seeking to be a chaste celibate must not suppress tenderness and emotion while seeking to avoid pregenital or genital behavior. As in most areas of human accomplishment, advance is along a knife-edge, avoiding on the one hand an unrealistic puritanism and on the other an indulgence of inappropriate behavior which is disguised as virtue. I have come to suspect both the angelic battle of the 1940s and the "third way"[2] of the 1970s as being denials of sexual reality.

The chaste single Christian must live with sexual drives and needs, fantasies and temptations, and perhaps at times feelings of anger and frustration because a call from God has thwarted the fulfillment of so powerful a drive. Self-pity will be of no use and is dispelled by the recognition that all human beings cope with drives that they cannot or should not fulfill.

Who can live a healthy life and totally satiate the appetite for food? Who can express anger and annoyance without limitation? Who can lead a life of indulgence in any pleasure without restraint?

Can anyone irresistibly cater to the sexual drive and be a well-balanced person? The chaste single person must be able to use more restraint and tolerate more frustration of this appetite. He or she must be something of an ascetic, who consciously moderates all appetites, and substantially restrains one, namely, sexuality.

Intimacy and the Single Life

The great question that faces the single person is intimacy. Must the single person be a loner, someone with repressed emotions and bottled-up feelings, expressing little warmth and affection? When the question is put in this way, even the most sober puritan of the first half of this century would answer, "Of course not."

Still, the interesting and disturbing question remains: Does the chaste single person, religious or lay, have to avoid relationships of

---

2. For those unfamiliar with this term, the third way became a short-hand term for the theory that those vowed to chastity could engage in deep emotional relationships with the opposite sex with no real danger to their commitment.

intimacy and affection which may move toward sexual expression? Many contemporary writers would enthusiastically say no. I'd be inclined to say "sometimes no and sometimes yes." Admittedly this is a more challenging answer, and it will annoy those who like easy solutions, especially in an area as imprecise as psychosexual needs. But challenging answers to complex questions are what make life interesting. Let's see what we can do to clarify this apparent ambiguity.

The need for intimacy and emotional support is as complex as the sexual drive is simple. Observations of the birds and the bees will indicate that the fulfillment of genital need is the simplest thing in the world. Even among human beings, sexual acts as well as sexual relationships are readily available to the most thoughtless and undiscriminating.

The need, however, for affection and personal intimacy is very complex. The infant learns to express this need very early on. Behavioral scientists have observed that distortions in fulfilling the need for affection and love in infancy may lead to disaster later on. The child needs all kinds of affection and emotional reinforcement if it is to grow. The affective needs of infants and children are devoid of direct sexual expression in the adult sense of the term.

In the teenager's experience only some affective relationships may have sexual overtones. He will love his male friends one way, and his girlfriends in another. Even the teenage boy with homosexual tendencies will be able to experience affection for women, although he experiences little or no sexual attraction to them. The same is true of the girl with homosexual tendencies.

All reasonably balanced human beings experience non-sexual attraction and affective responses toward others. Members of our own family, older people, children, persons who are not sexually attractive, friends—all may be objects of our strong need for affection and response. When they respond warmly to our need for them, they may never stir the slightest sexual attraction.

It was an illusion of Sigmund Freud—an illusion that cost him many of his most devoted disciples—that all attraction is libidinous and based on disguised sexual need. Few people in the behavioral sciences today take Freud's pan-sexualism seriously, although many, including myself, suspect that all affective need for others, sexual or non-sexual, grows out of the single, undifferentiated experience of the infant.

Although we all have close relationships which are clearly non-sexual, the most challenging are the affective relationships which may have some sexual components. It is obvious that a person who has chosen to be chaste and single for any of the reasons given in Chapter 2 must avoid close relationships which normally lead to sexual, and eventually to genital, expression. Most of us have friends who are or could be sexually attractive to us. It does not take much imagination to realize that such friendships could lead to the desire for direct sexual expression, if restraint were not used in all aspects of the relationship.

The most obvious example of the need for restraint and the subtle ways in which it is observed is friendship between married couples of the same age. Presumably the opposite partners could easily be sexually attractive to each other. In such "couple friendship," it is easy to observe that subtle proprieties and restraints are very quickly employed.

The single celibate is in a more difficult position regarding friends who are sexually attractive. First of all celibate life demands much more sexual control than married life ordinarily does. Expressions of affection may move easily into sexual fantasy. If a person has always led a chaste life, then fantasy is stronger because sexuality still has a mythological aura about it. Abstinence may accidentally feed unrealism. This has caused many religious celibates to withdraw from a wide range of human relationships which could possibly have sexual components.

A single person seeking to avoid any relationships where sexual attraction may occur will soon be painted into a very tight corner.

On the other hand, single persons who engage in close, emotionally expressive relationships with sexually attractive friends will often find themselves on the way to marriage, or at least having an affair. Many proponents of the "third way" for celibates found themselves exactly in this position.

Perhaps this complex challenge may be summarized best by a few practical suggestions. This is especially appropriate, since we rarely encounter these problems theoretically; we confront them in everyday life.

1. The single person should cultivate a wide variety of relationships, some of which are obviously intimate and affectionate. These should include relationships with family and friends and perhaps with a few people who could be sexually attractive. Many lonely people fail to realize that friendships have to be cared for and cultivated like plants in a garden. If you think you should be loved just because you are you, you missed your vocation. You should have been God.

2. At least one intimate friend, preferably a few, are needed in every life. If you want to be at peace and chastely celibate, it is wise to form friendships with people who are not sexually attractive to you. Otherwise, life gets too conflicted. Intimate friendships with sexually attractive persons usually lead to some sexual expression or conflict.

3. If a celibate person has sexually attractive friends, a proportionate amount of circumspection is needed. Manipulation, subtle forms of seductiveness, and exclusiveness should be avoided. An honest person should be humble enough to admit when seductiveness has accidentally entered a relationship. If one really intends to remain single, it is hardly a form of love to play with a friend's affection or life.

4. The most powerful friendship may be formed with a "companion on the inner way." This relationship, so well described by Morton Kelsey, is of particular importance for a

chaste single person.[3] What is more engaging than meeting others on the spiritual journey, which St. Augustine calls the longest journey, the trek to the interior Sinai?

True spiritual companions must always accept that God has first claim on our love. These friendships of their own nature should not be exclusive or manipulative. One should have several spiritual companions if possible. If it should happen that one has some sexual attraction, the friendship need not be terminated, but honesty and singleness of intention (properly called purity of heart) must always be preserved. When spiritual companionship moves into a sexual relationship outside marriage, those involved may do a great deal of harm to themselves and others because they will be able to reinforce each other's defense mechanisms of denial and rationalization. Such friendships can survive, although the spiritual aspect will diminish. If, however, a person has previously resolved to be celibate, a profound conflict will be generated and someone will definitely be hurt.

Chaste Expressions of Sexuality

This phrase may startle you a little. We have come to link the words sexual and genital, implying involvement of the reproductive organs. The fact is that we express our sexual identity in the way we walk, talk, dress, work and recreate. Each person has the right to his or her own expression of self-image, unless, as in the case of Bluebeard or Jezebel, this expression is damaging to others.

If you are single, it may be worthwhile to take stock of yourself. Are you comfortable with who you are, or are you ill at ease and projecting a false image? While some single people dress and act seductively out of naiveté, others go through life in a kind of neuter mode, so that one is not sure whether they are man or woman. I am not referring to an overly assertive woman or overly

3. Morton Kelsey, *Companions on the Inner Way.* New York: Crossroad, 1983.

refined man, but to people who have opted to present themselves as a sexual zero. Such a situation suggests to me that unfortunately they are not at peace with their sexuality.

There is a special problem here for singles with homosexual tendencies. Those trying to lead a chaste life often suffer because they feel dishonest by not revealing their tendencies to others. They stay "in the closet." Yet their friends and relatives may not be prepared for them to reveal their tendencies directly. One man who had given up a very long homosexual career wrote to me as follows: "I am tired of being something I'm not. I am fed up with allowing two percent of my body to dominate the whole of my existence. I'm tired of thinking of myself as a homosexual. I'm not. I'm a person, and I owe it to myself to be a person—to be me."

For some reason clerics and religious in particular used to feel compelled to present the self as neuter. Most of the time this did not work, and anyone familiar with religious life knew that many were obviously comfortable with their genders, while they had their sexuality under good control. A reasonable acquaintance with the lives of saints who were religious reveals that these remarkable Christians were usually very clear in presenting their self-image.

What about the not-too-masculine man or the not-too-feminine woman? This is a real issue for singles in general, and for religious in particular. In the helping professions, among teachers, social workers, health care professionals and the clergy, most men have a well developed "anima," a feminine side, and many women seem to have a strong "animus," or masculine component, in their personality. This balance makes it possible for the individual to help others creatively. Anyone who finds a fairly strong component of the other gender in his or her personality simply has to be objective and careful with the presentation of self. It is certainly undesirable to communicate a confusing or conflicting message about one's own self-image.

A curious kind of passive aggression and self-rejection may develop in the overly gentle boy or the overly aggressive girl. They may be forced by others to dislike themselves. If this is compounded by an anxiety about homosexuality, then the person may become assertive in a self-destructive way. It seems to me that a great deal of posing and self-mocking—even the use of the word "gay"—are leftovers from a childhood or adolescence filled with self-hate. This damaging propensity is really a form of self-punishment which does not make a single life easier or more productive.

One of the clichés of pop psychology is that everyone should be comfortable with his or her sexuality. Such a statement is probably a description of the world before the Fall. Very few people under seventy-five (some say ninety) are all that comfortable with their sexuality. It is too complex and powerful a force, so familiar and yet buried in the subconscious.

Everyone, including the chaste single person, consciously and intelligently, must try to integrate sexuality into the whole of life. Chastity is an expression of sexuality. Insofar as it is not, mere sexual abstinence is an expression of repression and unrealism. Every mature person has to be realistic about sexuality, no one more so than someone trying to lead a chaste single life.

Preconscious Sexuality

Sexual desire, with or without tender emotions and a need for intimacy, is a part of every human life. The single person has to live with it, recognizing that sexual abstinence may cause the unconscious and preconscious mind to be more, rather than less, sexually active. It goes beyond the scope of this book to examine the relationship of the conscious, thinking and morally responsible person and the great dark inner sea of the unconscious. The study of this relationship is one of the great dramas of modern psychology; people who fail to recognize the profound issues involved frequently get hurt by an injudicious involvement in the unconscious, just as those unfamiliar with the sea often get drowned.

In Chapter 4 we will discuss how to deal creatively with the preconscious and the unconscious. For the present, it is sufficient to indicate that the chaste celibate, like everyone else, cannot expect to fathom intellectually or eliminate voluntarily the deep rivers of sexual desire or of the need for affection and intimacy. Only at the end of a long life of struggle can one hope to overcome the self-centered assertiveness which flows in many forms in the depths of the psyche. It is the task of spirituality to help us cope with these vast currents, not to attempt to dam them up. In these depths lie the profound energy systems of human existence, including the energy to follow God's call to holiness.

In these depths, also, lurk the most dangerous effects of original sin, some innate and some derived from the environment. A failure to recognize and deal with the unconscious may lead to catastrophe. The following observation on the "shadow," a term that represents the unconscious part of the psyche containing both negative and positive aspects, was made by Frances G. Wickes, an American psychologist of the Jungian school who has long been interested in the spiritual life.

> Sometimes when one feels that the obstacles of life even when faced with courage are insurmountable, one may discover that part of the difficulty is caused by the unsuspected activity of the "shadow."[4]

Wickes discussed the case of a man who, out of a sense of propriety, had suppressed these mysterious and disturbing feelings into a polite silence in order to have an appropriately harmonious environment. She then made the following observation about the effects of such denial:

> Realities dwindle when one fears anything which might disturb surface calm, whether these realities are in the outer situation or the inner. Then the difficulties may be projected. The devil is at work in the other fellow. The shadows of others fall across the path and they must be

---

4. *The Choice Is Always Ours*, ed. Phillips, Howes, Nixon. Wheaton, Ill.: Quest Books, 1972 (originally published by Harper & Row, 1966), pp. 309–310.

avoided. The outer life narrows, the inner life becomes
more shallow. But, down below, the Shadow has a good
supper.[5]

The importance of dealing with preconscious sexuality and the
intelligent engagement of the shadow is illustrated by the following
case history. The facts of this case are as given, although some
details have been changed.

Edward was a devout and intelligent seminarian within two years
of ordination to the priesthood. He came from what any pastor
would have seen as an ideal home. His parents were devout, hard-
working and educated. They worked together to give their
children all that they could, and to prepare them for this world and
the next. Ed's single goal in life was to be a missionary.

Chastity was a serious value in his life and he believed that he was
well prepared to live a chaste life. His parents had provided
adequate instruction on "the facts of life." His older brothers and
sisters were already married and he had been aware of their
experiences as they prepared for marriage. Ed had a very strong
conscience, which a theologian could admire for its intellectual
content and its power to direct his behavior. A psychologist would
have detected a tendency to see things too much as black or white,
a tendency described as a rigid super ego. But Ed compensated in
many ways for his apparent rigidity. He was concerned about
others, involved in social issues and genuinely sympathetic to the
needs of the unfortunate. The only one that Ed was ever hard on
was himself.

One summer Ed was assigned to work in a very poor area. To his
own horror he became involved with two different girls his own
age. Both girls were experienced with sexuality. Neither of them
was shocked or scandalized at Ed's behavior because they felt sorry
for him. "He was such a nice guy and he seemed to know so little
about life." This was their attitude.

---

5. *Ibid.*, p. 310.

Ed took a year off from the seminary and worked in a social agency. His behavior went out of control, although his conscience and value system did not move at all. At my suggestion, he entered therapy with a religiously oriented psychologist. Ed also prayed fervently for help from God. Finally he concluded that the priesthood was not for him—he felt he could not live without sexual intimacy.

He is now married to a very devout woman and they have several children. Ed explained to me later that he had no choice but to marry. He felt that God had not answered his prayer for the grace to lead a celibate life and had consequently indicated that marriage was the road for him.

This is a disturbing case for people of several different ideologies. The devout will feel either that Ed was dishonest or that he did not belong in the seminary in the first place. I would challenge anyone to know this man and believe that.

Others will say that Ed's case suggests that mandatory celibacy for priests simply keeps good men out of the priesthood and should be abolished. The fact is that many men, with backgrounds similar to Ed's, are satisfied priests, functioning well and able to be chaste without any difficulty. On the other hand, others will say that Ed is bound to have an unhappy marriage since he married to solve his problems. But he is happily married. He and his wife are similar in many ways, and they have had a happy home for a number of years.

Ed's experience suggests to me that repression is a dangerous form of sexual control, especially when it is used exclusively to manage one's sexuality. Ed explained to me that whenever he was aware of the slightest sexual attraction or fantasy, he energetically put it from his mind. He was never troubled by temptations to auto-eroticism or to any other sexual expression. As far as chastity went, he had conquered all the worlds there were to conquer at the age of seventeen. He had few temptations at all, until the fateful day when the irresistible urge hit him.

The moral of this case history is that conscious control, with all the struggles that it implies, is a far better way to manage life than is repression, or forcing all impulses into the unconscious mind.

Although a fine person, Ed had never really assumed responsibility for his sexual behavior because he had never been challenged. When the challenge came, the power of repressed sexual feelings was so strong that it hit him like a tidal wave. Rather than gently taking responsibility for his behavior, Ed prayed and waited for a spiritual miracle—the removal of all sexual impulse. Again he did not take responsibility for himself. This can be done as it is done in Alcoholics Anonymous, even when one admits that one is powerless. Ed's mind and self-image were too rigid to make such an admission and to deal directly with such objectivity. If he had been able to cope with the idea that he was a poor weak sinner like everyone else, he might have groped through the challenges of his repressed needs and, with the grace of God, achieved conscious control.

The question may occur to you as it occurred to me: Why didn't he receive some special grace to get him over this hurdle? This question brings up the larger issue of God's Providence. Perhaps it was not to be. Ed had something stronger even than his virtue, and that was his faith. In all this darkness he believed that God would lead him to where he was supposed to be. When I visited Ed and his wife, I was sure that God had done so. If we believe, we give God the chance to write straight with crooked lines.

Attraction and Infatuation

We have already discussed relationships based on non-sexual attraction, and those which are only secondarily sexual. The single person must accept them calmly and intelligently. A word must be said about infatuation—a strong, emotional attraction. Such attraction is based on complementarity, a dynamic in which the strengths of one person respond to the needs of another. Complementarity may be seen as the very foundation of heterosexuality even on a physical level, where the physical characteristics which one sex lacks are most attractive to the opposite sex. Complementarity on a much more integrated level includes emotions, character traits and talents, and is the foundation of a good marriage.

Complementarity also operates in many non-sexual friendships. We are drawn to others partly because they resemble us, and also because they have what we lack, and need what we have in abundance. Some writers have used the term infatuation to describe the strong experience of such complementary relationships. I would prefer to restrict the term to that phase of relationship, usually short-lived, in which the other person is idealized as in romance or hero worship, or as in a superficial kind of discipleship.

Infatuation, which is complementarity in its most elementary form, must develop into a more realistic friendship which goes beyond complementarity, if it is going to endure. Meditating on the Gospel has led me to believe that in some ways the first disciples experienced infatuation with the Messiah, and that their relationship with Him had to be purified and transformed beyond hero worship. Such growth in awareness was a necessary part of their training which would be put to its ultimate test on Good Friday.

The single person must not be afraid of complementarity or infatuation, even the beginnings of sexual infatuation. But to maintain a chaste single life one must be very realistic and objective about such infatuating experiences, especially if sexual or romantic elements are hidden below the surface. In such non-sexual relationships as hero worship, the worst danger is that of looking like a fool. In sexual relationships, severe dislocation of two personalities may take place and a lot of harm may be done. The single person owes it to himself or herself to recognize infatuation and to grow beyond it quickly.

Sexual Compulsion and the Loss of Control

A single person must live with the possibility of sexual compulsions which are rooted in unconscious forces, or which stem from unresolved life crises. Sexual control is often the weakest link in an individual's personality and control system. When things go badly or when one is under great pressure, undesirable sexual behavior is likely to occur. The fear of losing sexual control often causes the single person a great deal of anxiety. Admittedly it will mark a further step in the development of our species when we are able to evaluate the loss of sexual control as symptomatic at times of inner strife, rather than always condemning it as the acting out of a simple immoral impulse, or, even more dangerous, justifying it by dishonest rationalization.

The loss of sexual control leads to undesired behavior that the individual sees as immoral and wishes to avoid. This is a special danger for the single person. Many of the control mechanisms present in marriage are simply not available in the single life. Hammarskjöld made the following observation in *Markings:*

> So, once again, you chose for yourself—and opened the door to chaos. The chaos you become whenever God's hand does not rest upon your head.
>
> He who has once been under God's hand, has lost his innocence: only he feels the full explosive force of destruction which is released by a moment's surrender to temptation.
>
> But when his attention is directed beyond and above, how strong he is, with the strength of God who is within him because he is in God. Strong and free, because his self no longer exists.[6]

The fear of losing control in periods of stress is a great argument for trying to live a sane and balanced life if you are single. Later we shall see how mental habits are so necessary for maintaining sexual control and for general good balance.

Homosexual Tendencies

We have already suggested that a fair number of men and women remain single because of homosexual tendencies. A more detailed

---

6. *Markings.* New York: Alfred A. Knopf, 1966, p. 98.

discussion of this condition is called for here. If this is not of interest to the reader, please pass on to the last section of this chapter on the single life.

The Present Confusion

Throughout this book I will refrain from using the word *homosexual* as a noun. Even though I know a number of people with these tendencies, I will never say, "Joe is a homosexual." To me, Joe is a person. Although we use the verbal short-hand and say, "Sam is an alcoholic," or "Mary is a psychotic," I prefer to say, "So-and-so is a person with this or that tendency." God did not create alcoholics or psychotics, and I have never met anyone whom He made a homosexual. God made persons.

I frequently hear persons with homosexual tendencies say "God made me this way, so it must be all right." I believe that this is a rationalization. It may be a very understandable rationalization for someone torn in two by a profound conflict of sexual desire and moral obligation. For the moment it may even be a forgivable rationalization, but we do persons with homosexual tendencies no favor by giving them a big dispensation from the moral law, especially since we have no divine authority to do so. We who do the dispensing may put ourselves in greater moral jeopardy than those whom we excuse. It is not the job of a doctor or clergyman to tell someone that what is wrong is right, although it has been done many times in medical and ecclesiastical history.

The twentieth century did not discover homosexuality. Historians of this subject suggest that it has been an observable human phenomenon since classical antiquity. Homosexual behavior is forbidden in both the Old and New Testaments and in early Christian writings. It has been consistently recognized as contrary to the moral code of the Christian world.

I am convinced that the person with a strong homosexual attraction, and even with a homosexual life-style reinforced by years of sexual activity (if you will, a homosexual identity), is called to a chaste life. However, this may not be a realistic expectation until the individual is prepared to respond to the grace of moral conversion. Leanne Payne in *The Broken Image* gives several examples of persons deeply immersed in homosexuality who, by the power of God's grace, have come to lead chaste Christian lives.[7] My experience with homosexually oriented Christians seeking a way out of their difficulty is similar to Dr. Payne's.

Homosexuality—Pseudo- and Real

It is the impression of many psychologists and psychiatrists, including Irving Bieber, who have worked primarily with homosexually oriented people during their professional careers, that many homosexually oriented persons are really latently heterosexual.[8] Because of fear of their own heterosexuality growing out of some childhood trauma, they are attracted to someone of their own sex as a veiled substitute for a person of the opposite sex.

For instance, a young man may be frightened or repelled by the aggressive masculinity of his schoolmates. He is shocked to hear them speaking of their sexual exploits with girls. He is repelled by this expression of masculinity and rejects part of his own identity. Not long after he may meet another male who has had the same experience. Sharing a repulsion at this crude expression of heterosexuality, they accept the less aggressive, more gentle exchange of homosexual acts. This explains why male "homosexuals" are often rather gentle, unaggressive persons.

A girl with homosexual tendencies may have gone through a slightly different trauma. She may have seen male sexuality as crude or, at best, unattractive. She may even have been forced into a heterosexual act. The aspect of femininity that is attractive to men may be frightening or revolting to her. The girl meets another

7. Leanne Payne, *The Broken Image*. Westchester, Ill.: Crossway Books, 1981.

8. Irving Bieber, *et al.*, *Homosexuality—A Psychoanalytic Study of Male Homosexuals*. New York: Vantage Books (Alfred A. Knopf).

girl who is equally frightened by heterosexual acts and they become partners without the fear and shame that they have come to associate with heterosexual behavior. I consider the persons in each case to be latent, but frightened, heterosexuals, or "pseudo-homosexuals."

Another kind of pseudo-homosexuality is quite common, in which a person was unloved or loved wrongly as a child. A pathological self-love begins to develop called "narcissism," after the lonely Greek shepherd boy who fell in love with his own reflection in a pool. Believing that he saw a god, he jumped into the pool and drowned in the illusory embrace of his own reflection and later returned to earth as a flower. We all have a touch of narcissism left over from childhood, and so we should be sympathetic toward someone who is driven to find another image of himself or herself.

In more healthy relationships, the residual narcissism of childhood is at least tacitly recognized and integrated among healthier factors of a good relationship, such as that between teacher and student. In severe cases the unfortunate person is driven to go through life clutching at and embracing someone who is a symbolic image of their idealized self. They never find this image, since there is no one who is their other self, and they go through a series of infatuations ending in emotional disaster.

At times the added problem of age may enter in. An older person may be seeking himself as a child or adolescent in someone considerably younger. Or a younger person may be driven to look for a loving parent of the same sex who was emotionally absent or unavailable in childhood.

Another theory on the origins of pseudo-homosexual impulses should be mentioned. Eli Siegal maintained that men with homosexual tendencies had mothers who gave their affection too easily, even seductively, causing these men to hold the affection of women in contempt.

It is my impression that none of the above cases represent a basic homosexual inversion, properly termed "syntonic homosexuality."

The homosexual tendencies described so far are simply not an inherent part of the personality; rather, they result from some accident in childhood. They are alien to the personality, or "dystonic." Consequently, the persons described will always be frustrated, always looking for the golden boy or girl, until life has dealt them so many disappointments that they simply stop in their tracks, or continue to seek any kind of sexual release. This, I am told, is unfortunately a familiar picture in the "gay scene."

Syntonic homosexuality flows from the very depths of the personality. I believe that in most, if not all, cases, this is represented by the person who really wants to belong to the opposite sex. This, if one cares to use the term, is real homosexuality. It occurs in the case of a man who profoundly wants to be a woman, and vice versa. The technical term for this is transsexualism. In recent decades attempts have been made through surgery to deal with this problem, but there is no significant evidence that such procedures have done anything to alter the individual's personal, psychological conflicts.[9] Knives rarely solve psychological conflicts, much less spiritual ones.

In all the above cases I suggest that a life of chaste celibacy may be the answer. Proposing such a life may seem very far-fetched to someone who has made homosexual behavior an integral part of life adjustment. But many people who have made heterosexual acts part of their life adjustment have learned to live without genital sexuality, as in the case of widows, divorced persons, and those who have entered religious life after living as adults with no commitment to celibacy or chastity. The present tragic epidemic of AIDS has caused many people to consider the possibility of a life of sexual abstinence with no other motivation than survival.

If you have homosexual tendencies and a reinforced pattern of homosexual behavior, you may be very tired of the whole thing. I

---

9. Cf. Anthony Mastroeni, *A Moral Evaluation of Surgical Sex-Reassignment.* Rome: University of St. Thomas (Angelicum), 1981. Fr. Mastroeni's dissertation reviews this question very thoroughly.

have heard dozens of homosexually oriented men and women say that a chaste life was far more desirable than the constant search for the perfect partner, that other self who does not exist (Narcissus who never is there). People grow weary of being rejected, or of being apparently accepted and then thrown away.

Not long ago I spoke to a twenty-year-old man who had recently informed his parents that he was "gay" and was going to follow that life-style. His father was doubly upset because he realized that his own alcoholism, now arrested, had contributed to the boy's problems in his teens. I realized that my suggestion of a chaste single life with a possible relinquishment of pseudo-homosexual identity through psychotherapy was not at all an appealing prospect to this young man. I prayed for guidance to the Holy Spirit, and then heard myself saying to him, "You are not ready to listen to me now, but someday, maybe ten or twenty years from now, you will be ready. You will be tired of it all. Remember that you once met a priest who told you there was another way. But it will require courage to take it."

The Single Life—A Simple but not an Easy Answer
The thought has probably crossed your mind that you never knew that being single was such a complicated vocation. Actually, the complexities arise from sexuality, not from chastity. For the Christian a chaste marriage or a chaste single life is one of the simplest solutions to the complexities of human sexuality. Once chastity is rejected, life gets very turbulent as the music, drama and literature of the world will attest.

Chastity, and indeed the practice of any virtue, will simplify life's choices and the consequences of these choices, leaving the individual free to carry the easy yoke and the light burden of Jesus Christ. But it would be, so to speak, a flaw in God's plan if, by practicing a virtue, we could walk into Utopia. The disciple would never grow, but would remain at the level of those naive and childish religious who appeared in the films of the 1940s and 1950s.

To be a Christian is simple in the sense that it is not complicated, but it requires the use of intelligence to gain insight and free will to accept the call of grace. We would never try to follow God's call unless He first called us. St. Augustine, who broke free from a life of illicit sexual indulgence, described in poetic language the experience of one called by God to chastity after a life of sin.

> Late have I loved Thee, O Beauty so ancient and so new; late have I loved Thee! For behold Thou wert within me, and I outside; and I sought Thee outside and in my unloveliness fell upon those lovely things that Thou hast made. Thou wert with me and I was not with Thee. I was kept from Thee by those things, yet had they not been in Thee, they would not have been at all. Thou didst call and cry to me and break open my deafness: and Thou didst send forth Thy beams and shine upon me and chase away my blindness: Thou didst breathe fragrance upon me, and I drew in my breath and do now pant for Thee: I tasted Thee, and now hunger and thirst for Thee: Thou didst touch me, and I have burned for Thy peace.[10]

---

10. St. Augustine, *Confessions*, X, XXVII, *op. cit.*, pp. 188–189.

Part 2

Suggestions for a Chaste Single Life

4

Sexual Problems of Single Persons and Some Solutions

We have already described how non-genital expressions of sexuality must be a legitimate part of life for every chaste single person. It remains to discuss the more common problems which occur when sexual behavior becomes illicit, that is, contrary to the moral law and the individual's conscience. Solutions to these problems can be immediate and related to specific behavior, or remote and comprehensive, affecting the individual's whole lifestyle personally and spiritually.

In this chapter we will turn our attention to specific problems and immediate solutions. In Chapter 5 we will look at more comprehensive answers and at the quality of life necessary to preserve a resolution of chastity. In Chapter 6 we will consider what psychology can tell us about fantasies, temptations, failures and successes in the effort to be a chaste single person. Finally, in Chapter 7 we will look at the spiritual side of this endeavor and the essential ingredients of Christian discipleship which expresses itself in a chaste life.

The Good and Broken Resolution

Many single Christians, and indeed most people trying to lead good lives despite self-centeredness and cupidity, find that good resolutions alone do not guarantee virtuous behavior. The good resolution is a start, but, as St. Augustine points out, we are often

57

at war with ourselves, struggling to die to death and yet hesitating to live to life.

Let us assume that everyone reading this book has made good resolutions and is pursuing some of them right now. If, after having made a serious resolution for chastity, the single person continues to have difficulties, the problems will probably fall into the following categories:

1. Sexual involvement in which affection and intimacy are components, that is, with a friend or a lover. We will refer to such people as those *by love possessed*.
2. Sexual involvement with persons who are not affectively linked to the individual and may even be anonymous. This is a kind of object sexuality which I have called *the wolf of the steppes*, borrowing a phrase from Herman Hesse.
3. Auto-eroticism or symbolic sexuality: I will refer to this problem as *the lonely passion*.
4. Sexual deviation which has been described to some extent above. I have characterized it here as *the scarlet letter*.

By Love Possessed

Despite good resolutions and frequently as a result of neurotic need and self-indulgence, a person who has decided to remain single may "fall in love." Powerful forces of intimacy, need, affectivity and loneliness may cause a relationship of friendship to become genitally expressed, often in spite of the resolutions of the individuals involved.

When I looked for a phrase to describe the condition in which a person is in love against previously accepted precepts or commitments (for instance, as in adultery, in the abandonment of religious vows, in the contradiction of the resolution of a single person to remain chaste), I was originally going to term it "Love gone wrong." But this is inaccurate since in almost all these situations there is genuine human affection rather than simple lust, and the word "wrong" can be misleading. True love is not wrong insofar as it is true, because it is part of the virtue of charity. So I chose a phrase from fiction to suggest that a particular human love is so possessive that it prevents a person from being free and chaste. There is nothing wrong with one man loving another man's wife as a chaste friend, but if the love sexualizes and becomes controlling, he is by love possessed against his own moral convictions.

Apart from the fact that love genitally expressed outside marriage is morally wrong, there are also other defects in it. Anyone going against his moral convictions will almost always use extensive denial and rationalization. These are common defense mechanisms, or unconscious distortions of reality. In other words, they are lies we tell ourselves. I have often heard people who had lived sensitive Christian lives of service simply ignore this segment of their reality which was once of paramount importance to them. This is the meaning of the old saw that "love is blind." When sexualized human affection (erotic love) takes possession, a devoted spouse may be destroyed, children abandoned, a career of service demolished, scandal given—all in the name of "love."

Denial and rationalization are fed by fantasy. The single person is particularly vulnerable to this combination of distortions. An engaging but morally illicit relationship may lead to "playing house." Some years ago a visually beautiful and romantic film, *Elvira Madigan,* told of two young people, one of them married, who "fell in love" and spent a beautiful weekend together. The viewer was apt to forget the immoral circumstances in the apparently innocent expressions of love which were in no way gross or obscene. But the weekend and film ended abruptly with two gunshots as the couple committed suicide together. Playing house and playing at love often have catastrophic results.

The best solution to the problem of illicit love affairs is not to let them get started. This is true of both heterosexual and homosexual relationships. A friendship might be preserved if two people can keep it from pregenital expression. It is rare that it can be preserved after that, except when the two subsequently marry, and even then they may not be friends for long.

Once the friendship has become genitally expressed, chastity can be bought back only at a great price. At times two well-integrated people can agree to support each other in their efforts to be chaste. If this fails (and it often fails quickly), separation is the only answer. Time heals many wounds, and so do prayer and work. But deep wounds require much time, prayer and work.

A single person going through such a separation often makes the mistake of giving up something very powerful and replacing it with nothing. It is like stepping out of the window of a plane in the air. A wise person will seek the support of caring friends with whom the situation is shared. A recommitment to one's life of faith and prayer—perhaps during a short retreat—is very effective. Then the entire life situation of the individual should be objectively reviewed with a spiritual director to determine what spiritual and psychological support systems were missing, thereby causing the initial resolution to chastity to crumble.

Finally, the individual needs to make a whole new start in life, including, if advisable, a new work situation or new living accommodations. The spiritual components of a chaste single life must be constantly strengthened by prayer, generous work and a more intense use of the sacraments.

An interesting illustration of this problem comes to mind. Some years ago a priest sought me out to discuss the fact that he was in love with a religious sister. He was a dedicated and hard-working man, interested in prayer and the spiritual life, and so I was not surprised to learn that there had been no sexual involvement. Far from it. In fact he had never even told the sister that he was strongly attracted to her. He kept about his work and saw the sister only when duty occasionally brought him to the convent to offer the liturgy.

The sister sought him out for spiritual advice. At first he was frightened, but after prayer he decided it was best not to let his

problems or needs interfere with pastoral responsibilities. He gave
what counsel was called for and responded simply in a friendly
fashion. He knew that the sister was a deeply spiritual person and
that her associates almost venerated her saintly qualities. The
priest recognized indeed that it was partly these qualities that
made her so attractive to him. Only once, on a day of special
tragedy, did he even exchange a kiss with the sister. This
happened in the presence of several other people and was very
much an expected part of the situation.

The priest often thought of what it would be like to be married,
have a family and even have the sister as his wife.

But suddenly the sister was gone. She died of a rapid terminal
illness, and she never knew at all of the spiritual conflict that had
gone on in the soul of her friend. The priest, however, told me
that once he had been through this trial, he was more at peace
with a celibate vocation and had come to see it as a blessing that
God had given to him.

The Wolf of the Steppes

I have derived this term from Hesse's tragic figure of the man
driven to seek lonely and fleeting pleasures like a solitary wolf on
the plains. How many good people, single and married, have I
known who, in spite of their best intentions, have found
themselves in this lonely and forlorn position?

Although the driven seeking of anonymous sexual release is a
particular problem of the single, it is by no means a difficulty
unique to them. It can happen to the premarried and the married,
to the housewife and the father of a family, both of whom may love
their spouse. It can happen to a person in vows who woefully
regrets this failure in the service of God, but who feels compelled
to it by the clutch of an iron claw.

The anonymous seeking of sexual gratification from strangers is
usually pathetic, frustrating and humiliating, not to say dangerous

to reputation or even to life. Such driven sexual indulgence is often so regretted before, during and after the behavior that, as a confessor, I have come to attach much less moral importance to the act than to the responsibility of reorganizing one's life properly before the temptation arises again.

To understand this problem it is necessary to know that it is in some way linked to a desperate and subconscious need for intimacy often arising from early life experiences. It is a return to being a small child who needs to be embraced and loved in a physical way. Sometimes it is linked to very immature expressions of sexual need reminiscent of the naughty games children play behind the garage. Finally there is frequently a self-destructive element in such activity which drives the person to regression, humiliation and danger.

This behavior usually becomes a compulsion, that is, a pleasure that produces an irresistible need to do something one knows will be self-destructive. Like any compulsion, sexual compulsion becomes very powerful in a short time, and it can make its demands felt on a daily basis, destroying all integrity and order in a person's life, leaving the individual uneasy and deeply dissatisfied. The Freudian description of a compulsion as the pleasure principle (Id) in the service of the Super Ego (the primitive principle of self-punishment) seems valid indeed.

In most cases the sexual behavior to which one is driven is morally wrong and forbidden; yet, if one looks at the individual case, there is very little freedom left and, consequently, little enough real sin. As in the case of a drug addict or alcoholic, however, objective moral teaching provides some kind of guide—a lighthouse in a hurricane—so that the individual has some hope of being delivered eventually. It does not help to ignore a lighthouse in a hurricane, even if you can't get to it. Nor is it wise to ignore the moral law, even though you feel you haven't the strength to observe it.

The single person who is drawn to fleeting sexual pleasures and has not yet established an overwhelming compulsion must recognize the dangers involved and try, with the help of an informed confessor, counselor or therapist, to uncover some of the unconscious motivation. Words are often not enough. The person needs to arrive at a profound sense of the self-destructiveness and infantilism of such behavior. If a compulsion has already been established, it is essential to get professional or experienced help.

The support of a group similar to AA is most helpful. "Courage," to which I have referred previously, is such a group. The members support one another in their attempts to lead a chaste life in the face of strong homosexual tendencies, which in most cases had become part of their life-style. It is my hope that the Courage movement, which has many counterparts in the American Protestant community, will begin to spread throughout the Catholic Church.

The steps in overcoming a compulsion are very well summarized in the *Twelve Steps of Alcoholics Anonymous*. The first step is essential: admitting that one is powerless in the face of the compulsion and can be delivered only by the power of God. Equally important is an honest moral inventory. My suggestion to persons with compulsions is to attend some open AA meetings and take the steps with the help of a friend, preferably someone who has recovered from a sexual compulsion. They should also pay close attention to what we suggest in the following chapters of this book.

In looking for an example of a person trying to work through a compulsion, my problem was to pick one out of so many people with whom I have worked. I obtained permission from a friend to use the following description of his compulsive problem with only a few details changed.

Andy grew up in a devout home where his mother clearly was the dominant member of the family. He was a rather gentle soul and kept away from fights and anything aggressive. He decided early in life to be a priest. He went through the seminary without much difficulty and, in fact, fit in very well. His only serious problem

was that he found himself drawn to look at male genitals. At first
he had no attraction for any homosexually oriented friendship. He
simply excluded the strange attraction from the rest of his life,
which was both hard-working and prayerful. But when traveling,
out of the blue as it were, he would find himself in a public
restroom, at times involved in the most personally humiliating
activity. He was filled with remorse and guilt.

It took some months of counseling for him to accept this
compulsion for what it was: a form of symbolic behavior which
arose from a combination of loneliness, frustration and self-hate.
Following the basic outline of the twelve steps of Alcoholics
Anonymous, he was able to overcome this problem entirely. He
can scarcely believe that this was once part of his life, although he
is still very cautious after several years. He realizes that he was
fortunate, since such compulsions are often broken only after
irreparable harm has been done to one's reputation.

It is worth noting in this case that the person was always highly
motivated to recover; he never pretended that this was not both a
moral evil and a psychological problem, and he was a hard-working
and prayerful person. He purposely fought all tendencies toward
self-pity and self-hate, especially by a daily holy hour in the
presence of the Blessed Sacrament.

The Lonely Passion

What is more conflicted or sad than auto-eroticism or solitary
sexuality? The only positive thing one can say about auto-eroticism
is that it is a common phenomenon, and, since misery likes
company, the only consolation it offers is that one is not alone. It is
a problem that single people are especially likely to experience,
and one that is apt to occur particularly in times of loneliness,
stress, or anxiety. I use the word auto-eroticism intentionally,
rather than masturbation, to differentiate the former problem from
involuntary actions in sleep or semi-sleep, and also from childish
and early adolescent sexual behavior in which the youngster may
not really be said to have arrived at the psychological stage where

he may properly be called auto-erotic. He or she is simply immature.

I refer here to the activity of an older adolescent or adult who for a variety of reasons is driven in on self and finds a substitute for real living in this symbolic and intensely frustrating behavior. The most common excuse for this behavior is sexual release, or an attempt at defusing sexual frustration. In auto-eroticism, however, the person moves into fantasy and becomes involved in sexual desire. In sexual fantasy, which, like a dream, is a projection of the id or pleasure principle, there are no restrictions of propriety, morality or reason. Sexual fantasy may quickly become gross, obscene or deviant, something that is unlikely to happen in the sexual act with a spouse or lover.

Perhaps a pejorative word like "dirty," which is used to characterize sexual sin, arises from auto-erotic fantasy. Such a term is unsuitable when illicit sexuality takes place between those who have affection for each other. But it may easily fit the experience of indulged sexual fantasy where sexuality is pure lust, that is, the seeking of pleasure for its own sake. A pejorative term also fits the experience of anonymous sexual encounter. I have known of several instances in which those involved in an anonymous sexual situation completely lost all desire after a few words of communication. Lust may not survive where there is even a slight relationship, but it is always very powerful in auto-eroticism.

Other common motives for auto-eroticism include boredom, loneliness and self-hate. If the person is still deeply involved in unresolved narcissism with childish and regressive feelings, he or she is likely to be plagued by auto-eroticism. The single person suffering with this difficulty needs a good spiritual friend and an encouraging confessor with whom to discuss the problem. A good resolution may not be enough to end this practice; it may be necessary to adopt a number of changes suggested in the following chapters.

The great tragedy of a life marred by auto-eroticism is not that the individual is likely to destroy his or her relationship with God by serious sin. Because of human weakness there may, in fact, be no serious sin. It is true that the Church has taught for centuries that auto-eroticism is seriously wrong. Christ our Lord was very clear in His teaching that sin lies in desire, and what is the fantasy of auto-eroticism but lustful desire? As most confessors know, however, many sincere people, married and single, old and young, fall into this difficulty—evidently against their will. Most, if not all, sincere Christians with this problem want to be rid of it for good.

The tragedy of auto-eroticism, like that of any compulsive behavior, is that it sets the individual against himself and, apparently, against God. The person feels apart from God, and for very good reason. He or she has done something forbidden and has engaged in thoughts and desires contrary to the goodness of human nature which reflects the image of God. If one intends to be a disciple of Christ, it is absurd to try to square the inner production of X-rated fantasies with that discipleship. The pain of the person trapped in auto-eroticism is all the greater because he knows that despite his revulsion, there is some consent in the back of his mind to what the Lord has forbidden.

The forces of self-hate in auto-eroticism cannot be overemphasized. Perhaps it is the force of unbridled sexual fantasy that makes the shame and self-hate so powerful. In order to overcome this compulsion the help of another person is usually necessary—someone who can give the troubled individual an opportunity to be accepted with this dark secret.

I received the following letter from a young man I shall call Bill. He was a senior in college and was hoping to pursue a religious vocation. The intensity of compulsion suggested to him that he was dealing with a force beyond himself. This very poignant letter should be an invitation for all of us to be understanding.

> Tonight, while trying to fall asleep, I had a battle. I had a great deal of anxiety. As usual I had lustful thoughts with much guilt. The evil side of me was saying how I would like to spend this summer. It said, "I would like to have one big

long orgy with both sexes, and then at the end of the summer, in guilt and self-righteousness, I would like to quietly kill myself." This was satanic. Then my spirit thought of how much good I could do for my family if only I would get my act together. Of course I am sure this is wrong and only part of being passive-aggressive. Somehow I feel, if I am good, my family will not have as many problems as it does. So then when I am bad, I feel all the more guilty. But I did get to feel more peaceful as I thought of what I would say this week to the class I teach as a volunteer. Thursday will be our last class for the sixth grade. I thought: "I will teach them the importance of prayer." I got to feel much more quiet, and then I prayed.

Suddenly my lustful thoughts returned. I got out of bed and in a frenzy I yelled inside myself to Satan and to God, "I want no part of you, God, or you, Satan. Why don't you both leave me alone? I didn't ask to be made. Why do you both fight over me? I wonder if I will ever survive this fight! What will be left of me when you two are done?"

In the frenzy of all this the only thing that gave me consolation like a clearing in a storm was to think of what you said to me the last time you were here at the school and said goodbye. I was going past in the corridor when you called to me: "Come back here and say goodbye." Again and again just these words interrupted the storm within. "Come back and say goodbye."

Why didn't you just leave me alone? Why didn't you let me feel sorry for myself? It fills my eyes with tears to think that you are the only person to whom I feel safe in writing these things. Perhaps I don't tell these things to others because I try to be an angel or because of pride or because I don't want to torture others with my horrible feelings. But I tell you because it gives me some relief.

You tell me that these are only paper tigers, but paper cuts too. I mail this letter with great reservations. It is like tearing off a piece of myself and putting it in the mail. I really want to be part of God and his work, but sometimes I really don't know who I am.

Although in *The Confessions* St. Augustine is not explicit as to the
nature of the compulsion he struggled with, there is a strong
parallel between his experience and that of this young man.
Augustine, however, unlike the young man, does not speak of
frustration because of God's apparent failure to help him. Yet
anyone familiar with the saint's writing at this time of his life may
well suspect that he did in fact experience such feelings toward
God which gave rise to his later writings on humility.

The following excerpt sums up the painful conflict of someone
battling with a compulsion.

> Thus I was sick at heart and in torment, accusing myself
> with a new intensity of bitterness, twisting and turning in
> my chain in the hope that it might be utterly broken, for
> what held me was so small a thing! But it still held me. And
> You stood in the secret places of my soul, O Lord, in the
> harshness of Your mercy redoubling the scourges of fear
> and shame lest I should not be broken but should grow
> again to full strength and bind me closer even than before.
> For I kept saying within myself: "Let it be now, let it be
> now," and by the mere words I had begun to move toward
> the resolution. I almost made it, yet I did not quite make
> it. But I did not fall back into my original state, but as it
> were stood near to get my breath. And I tried again and I
> was almost there, and now I could all but touch it and hold
> it: yet I was not quite there, I did not touch it or hold it. I
> still shrank from dying unto death and living unto life. The
> lower condition which had grown habitual was more pow-
> erful than the better condition which I had not tried. The
> nearer the point of time came in which I was to become
> different, the more it struck me with horror; but it did not
> force me utterly back nor turn me utterly away, but held
> me there between the two.
>
>   Those trifles of all trifles, and vanities of vanities, my
> one-time mistresses, held me back, plucking at my gar-
> ment of flesh and murmuring softly: "Are you sending us
> away?" And "From this moment shall this or that not be

allowed you, now or forever?" What were they suggesting to me, O my God? Do You in your mercy keep from the soul of Your servant the vileness and uncleanness they were suggesting. And now I began to hear them not half so loud; they no longer stood against me face to face, but were softly muttering behind my back and, as I tried to depart, plucking stealthily at me to make me look behind. Yet even that was enough, so hesitating was I, to keep me from snatching myself free, from shaking them off and leaping upwards on the way I was called: for the strong force of habit said to me: "Do you think you can live without them?"[1]

The Scarlet Letter

I have borrowed this term from Nathaniel Hawthorne to characterize sexual deviations, not because they are the subject of his novel, but because they are often symbolic brand marks in a person's psyche. Sexual deviations fit Shakespeare's description of lust very well: "The expense of spirit in a waste of shame/Is lust in action; a bliss in proof—and prov'd, a very woe" (Sonnet 129).

A single person may be prey to some deviant desires or tendencies which may or may not be acted out, but which are always extremely distasteful. The catalogue of these frustrating tendencies is exhausting. They have been well documented by Otto Fenichel, one of Freud's most perceptive disciples.[2] To give them their due, the understanding of the mechanisms of deviation was a task at which the early Freudians excelled.

Without going into the tedious list of deviations, it is sufficient to say that a person may be compelled to such forms of sexual gratification because of inadequate psychological development. These acts may range from voyeurism (watching sexual scenes) to

---

1. *Confessions, op. cit.*, VIII, XI, pp. 139–140.
2. Cf. Otto Fenichel, M.D. *The Psychoanalytic Theory of Neurosis.* New York: W. W. Norton & Co., 1945. This book, while not for the general reader, may be helpful for those trained in psychotherapeutic methods.

sadism. Fetishism is perhaps the most common deviation after
voyeurism. It may involve touching the intimate apparel of another
person, or a situation or behavior which has no sexual significance
for others at all, such as touching a comb or eating fresh fruit. At
times it is possible to ascertain some sexual component in the
situation, and at other times it is not. Persons suffering from a
deviation have a special grief. They endure a terrible isolation with
their secret, which is their Scarlet Letter branded within. This is
especially true if the object of the deviation has no sexual
connotations for anyone else.

A single person who is trying to lead a chaste life may accidentally
exacerbate a deviation by going to extremes in order to avoid it.
This only highlights anxiety and strengthens the pull of the
deviation. On the other hand, the direct seeking of sexual pleasure
from the deviation always strengthens it, and at the same time it
will seriously damage the individual's self-image.

However difficult it may be, anyone struggling with a deviation
will find much release in sharing the problem with an informed
counselor or confessor, even if the desire has not led to sinful
behavior. Like paper tigers and ghosts, deviations are best looked
at in the daylight. I have found that a devout person who has been
very repressed in childhood will sometimes suffer from deviant
thoughts of a sado-masochistic type or be troubled by incestuous
desires. All of these are relieved when objectified in intelligent
and frank discussion. The more insight the individual gains into
the roots of the deviation, the more it will help him to control, or
perhaps even dispel it.

Hidden Occasions of Unchastity

Having considered the four most common forms of unchaste
behavior, we should round out our discussion by considering some
hidden occasions of sexual difficulty. These include some, like self-
pity, which are only extensions of more obvious factors like
narcissism, and some that are rarely ever considered, such as the
operation of malign influences external to the individual.

Self-Pity

When a person is filled with self-pity, even if the sentiment is somewhat justified by circumstances, there is a real possibility of regression or return to childish behavior. Sexual indulgence, especially auto-eroticism, is particularly common among those who are caught in self-pity. We all go through bouts of self-pity—what my Irish great-grandmother used to call "pity parties." However, serious and sensitive people—the very ones who are most likely to follow a call to a chaste celibate life—are particularly prone to self-pity. Without spouse or children to distract them, celibates are more likely to withdraw into self-pity. This is especially true if the chaste person tries to be patient and charitable all the time. There seems to be little left to do but put on a recording of "Clair de Lune" and wait for temptation to come. The one other alternative is to laugh at oneself and get out and do something for someone who has real problems.

Anger and Rage

A surprising number of good Christians are filled with a charge of anger at the world, at themselves and, ultimately, at God. Their anger is often deeply buried and shows itself as frustration and depression. It may also manifest itself in sexual activity in one of the four ways identified above. Sexual behavior of this type is usually self-punitive, causing the person to act in such a way that even the meager pleasure involved is painful.

In fact such a person is in the grip of a compulsion which is a distorted expression of sexuality. Usually the situation requires psychotherapy, so that the person may ventilate anger in appropriate ways and then gain insight into its real causes. Such persons need to realize that the quintessence of neurotic behavior is to act toward some symbol as if it were the real object of one's driven emotions. The self or some other person, or the Church, or perhaps the image of God, becomes the symbolic focus of an anger that is irrepressible and misdirected. The anger is frequently directed at parents who have often innocently made some mistake in raising their children.

Unexpected Love

It occasionally happens that two people encounter each other at a very painful or vulnerable point in their spiritual journey. This is done in all innocence when neither is seeking any sexual involvement. In fact they may not be sexually attracted to each other, but they are both experiencing some of the regression and emotional needs characteristic of one of the transition periods. For example, a relationship may develop between an older woman and a young man, or between two people of the same sex who are not at all inclined to homosexual attractions. What is really being experienced is a sudden and profound dependency at a time of psychological stress.

The support and counsel of loving friends may be crucial at this time. Direct explanation of what is going on along with an openness to insight may keep those who are bound by close emotional ties from moving toward any sexual expression. This will save a great deal of pain and shame for each person and may well preserve their friendship as a lasting value.

It may happen that only one of the persons in this situation is psychologically vulnerable and going through such a trauma. Then it is the responsibility of the other person to be generous and supportive, but well controlled. If this reasonable approach to the situation fails to control the emotionally disturbed person, withdrawal from the situation may be necessary. Someone trying to be a good Christian may feel guilty about such a tactic, but it may be necessary for the eventual psychological health of the other person.

The Dark Forces of Evil

For centuries, inside and outside Christianity, it has been common to blame the powers of darkness for sexual temptation and sin. As modern man becomes more understanding of the nature of the unconscious mind and of the complexities of the dynamisms of the mind, he tends to dismiss all reference to the forces of evil as obscurantist. This is a dangerous attitude, because we have been assured by St. Paul that our struggles are not only with flesh and blood, but against principalities and powers, against rulers of the world of darkness (Eph 6:12). Even those who believe in the existence of the powers of darkness tend to dismiss their activity as inconsequential and harmless to human beings. They fail to recall that Christ was betrayed because "Satan entered into Judas" (Jn 12:27).

There is no doubt that immense harm has been done to human beings by the abuse of sexuality. Untold suffering as well as much crime can be traced to forbidden sexual behavior even when such behavior was driven or performed in ignorance. Often this behavior is so damaging that one must stand back and ask whether the forces of evil, so often spoken of in Sacred Scripture, are not in some way responsible. Anyone inexperienced in these things should simply observe and keep the possibility in mind.

Anyone feeling oppressed or bothered by some outside force should be very careful not to relinquish responsibility for his own behavior. But he might be wise to pray for deliverance from any form of evil outside himself. The prayerful use of the sacraments in this case is very important.

Those who are experienced in helping people who are troubled by compulsions and sexual conflicts are likely to be open to the possibility of evil influences operating on a person. I know several devout people who have been through serious sexual conflicts. When confronted by pictures of the holocaust or some other episode of human atrocity, they have commented that they could recognize the malicious forces at work. There is no doubt that the twentieth century, while denying the existence of Satan, has provided many examples of behavior which could lead one to suspect the operation of such an influence. Human nature can't be that bad without help. [3]

---

3. Pope Paul VI encouraged Christians not to simply dismiss satanic influences as misunderstandings of the subconscious mind or other psychological processes. His powerful sermon "Deliver Us from Evil" (Nov. 15, 1973) and reprinted in *L'Osservatore Romano* (Nov. 23, 1973) is quoted in *Deliverance Prayer* by M. and D. Linn, S.J., New York: Paulist Press, 1980. This book will be helpful to all interested in the topic.

Those who are struggling to lead chaste celibate lives should not
be surprised by such obstacles. They must pray for both healing
and deliverance, preferably with others, and especially with
someone who appreciates their struggle.

He Will Rescue and Heal You

The long struggle against the sexual problems I have described can
be very discouraging to a good Christian, single or married. No
one ever said that being a disciple of Christ would always be
pleasant. There is, however, an aspect of the struggle which is
very encouraging: the realization that in striving to overcome these
problems, one is doing the work of God.

Christ encouraged his disciples to live by His Word and to know
the truth which would make them free. Every one of these sexual
tendencies, when surrendered to, is a departure from discipleship,
if not a betrayal. Every one of them involves the individual in the
denial of truth. They are all a flight into fantasy; they are unreal
lies one tells oneself about life and love. Ultimately they are all
false gods. A Christian who struggles to overcome them, even with
little apparent success, is doing the work of discipleship. The
Gospels clearly indicate that the apostles were not always
successful in their discipleship.

Perhaps you are saying, "Yes, I have tried, but I am tired of
failure." Perhaps you thought it was going to be easier than it
really is. You may have underestimated the power of the
subconscious, the wounds of childhood, and the unresolved
narcissism in your personality. It is possible that you never
thought about the special challenges of a vocation to continence,
with none of the genital expression of intimacy which is one of the
beauties of marriage.

St. Augustine, who went from a life of debauchery to a faithful
relationship with a single woman, and then to a life of chaste
celibacy, may have something to tell you about the severity of this
struggle, and about the power of grace and the message of

Scripture. It is well worth taking the time to meditate on the
following passage.

> When my most searching scrutiny had drawn up all my
> vileness from the secret depths of my soul and heaped it in
> my heart's sight, a mighty storm arose in me, bringing ₐ
> mighty rain of tears. That I might give way to my tears and
> lamentations, I rose from Alypius: for it struck me that sol-
> itude was more suited to the business of weeping. I went
> far enough from him to prevent his presence from being an
> embarrassment to me. . . . I arose, but he remained where
> we had been sitting, still in utter amazement. I flung myself
> down somehow under a certain fig tree and no longer tried
> to check my tears, which poured forth from my eyes in a
> flood, *an acceptable sacrifice to Thee.* And much I said not
> in these words but to this effect: *"And Thou, O Lord, how
> long? How long, Lord; wilt Thou be angry forever? Re-
> member not our former iniquities."* For I felt that I was still
> bound by them. And I continued my miserable complain-
> ing: "How long, how long shall I go on saying tomorrow and
> again tomorrow? Why not now, why not have an end to my
> uncleanness this very hour?"
>
>   Such things I said, weeping in the most bitter sorrow
> of my heart. And suddenly I heard a voice from some
> nearby house, a boy's voice or a girl's voice, I do not know:
> but it was a sort of sing-song repeated again and again,
> "Take and read, take and read." I ceased weeping and im-
> mediately began to search my mind most carefully as to
> whether children were accustomed to chant these words in
> any kind of game, and I could not remember that I had ever
> heard any such thing. Damming back the flood of my tears
> I arose, interpreting the incident as quite certainly a divine
> command to open my book of Scripture and read the pas-
> sage at which I should open. For it was part of what I had
> been told about Antony, that from the Gospel which he
> happened to be reading he had felt that he was being ad-
> monished as though what he read was spoken directly to
> himself: *"Go, sell what thou hast and give to the poor and*

thou shalt have treasure in heaven; and come follow me."
By this experience he had been in that instant converted to
You. So I was moved to return to the place where Alypius
was sitting, for I had put down the Apostle's book there
when I arose. I snatched it up, opened it and in silence read
the passage upon which my eyes first fell: *Not in rioting and
drunkenness, not in chambering and impurities, not in
contention and envy, but put ye on the Lord Jesus Christ
and make not provision for the flesh in its concupiscences.*
(*Romans* 8:13) I had no wish to read further, and no need.
For in that instant, with the very ending of the sentence,
it was as though a light of utter confidence shone in all my
heart, and all the darkness of uncertainty vanished
away. . . .

Then we went in to my mother and told her, to her
great joy. We related how it had come about: for she was
filled with triumphant exultation, and praised You who are
mighty beyond what we ask or conceive: for she saw that
You had given her more than with all her pitiful weeping
she had ever asked. For You converted me to Yourself so
that I no longer sought a wife nor any of this world's prom-
ises, but stood upon the same rule of faith in which You had
shown me to her so many years before. Thus You changed
her mourning into joy, a joy far richer than she had thought
to wish, a joy much dearer and purer than she had thought
to find in grandchildren of my flesh.[4]

---

4. *Confessions, op. cit.,* VIII, XII, pp. 141–142.

5

A Single Life With Style

Single people, especially the laity, are often made to feel like
second-class citizens, and they may begin to feel this way
eventually. Unfortunately, the single person facing life alone may
feel intimidated in a world of couples. There is often no one
waiting at the airport, no one with whom to discuss problems, no
one to call when you backed your car into a tree. The minor
emergencies of life frequently emphasize the single person's
vulnerability and lack of support. Everyone seeks help in major
emergencies. We all go to the hospital when we need surgery, but
the single person stays at home alone nursing a bad cold.

Many single people, aware of their private reasons for remaining
single, feel inferior because the real reasons are often not
flattering. (They ought to think about the reasons some people
have for getting married.) Since sexual problems of the type we
have discussed are often fed by self-pity, it is easy enough for a
single person to get into a vicious circle of self-hate and self-defeat.
It is the impression of some sociologists that the most vulnerable
person in American society is the middle-aged single man. The
single man may be most easily misunderstood, and in many cases
put in a bad light simply because he lives alone. This vulnerability
is largely founded on psychological attitudes which the single
generate for themselves.

It Is Not Good To Be Alone
Being single does not have to mean being alone. The single person
who wishes to lead a chaste life must make sure that he or she is

not alone too much. This requires an affirmative attitude about the value of having friends and friendly acquaintances. If you are single be sure that you are an active member of your neighborhood or the building you live in. Go to outings! Volunteer for things that require public spirit! You should definitely find a useful niche in your parish; if you cannot, join another parish.

The single person should belong to a club, or to a spiritual support group such as a Third Order, or a Christian community. The single person who smiles, is helpful and pitches in, is an asset to anyone trying to get a parish or neighborhood organized. Most clergy do fairly well as single people because they are part of many things by reason of their vocation. Isolated clergy and religious, on the other hand, often do poorly in their total life adjustment.

Single people should also cultivate a wide variety of friends. For them friends are more necessary than for those who are married. Singles make good friends of other singles of the same age. This is true of religious and priests as well. Making friends is an investment in time and interest. You may have friends who enjoy doing what you would never choose to do, but you go along anyway. Single men should know how to cook and invite single compatible acquaintances over for dinner. Single women who are worried about money for future security ought to spend a little of it now to enjoy and enrich their lives with their friends. The friends may be better security than a bank account.

The Extra Mile

The single person is also in a position to undertake special good works. An honest dedication to the poor and the needy is a great source of strength and personal satisfaction to many single people. Looking after the needy only from our own family can be a trap, however, for relatives can become overly dependent on the single person. It is best to spread charity far and wide and not waste too much time expecting recognition, especially from one's own family. If you want gratitude, buy a dog.

Finally, the single person should realize the need to give a bit more. Don't resent this or you will never be able to do it. You must go the extra mile especially in relationships with married friends and family.

Let me give an example. The annual family picnic is approaching, and mothers and daughters are preparing large platters of food. The single person can more easily bring some delicacy, a special cake or wine. There is little difference between the contributions in terms of labor and ingredients, but the cash outlay is more for the single person. Each family also contributes its own children to the day. Baby pictures and photographs of the latest wedding or graduation are passed around. Single people are expected to be interested in all of this, and if they are wise, they will show appropriate interest.

As an extra step, the single person might bring a game for the whole group to enjoy, or a bag full of colored balloons as decorations. Some will never notice the thoughtfulness, but some will. It is the difference between being Uncle Ed who was a quiet old bachelor (he was only fifty-six when he died), and Uncle Mike whom everybody loved and who sent everybody a birthday card. He never seemed to grow old. "Even though he was a bachelor, he was always so much fun." Take your choice. I suggest that since we pass this way but once, we should go first class.

The same is true of the widowed and the divorced, especially if their children have grown up. Put yourself out, go the extra mile, be an asset rather than a liability, an understanding friend rather than just another face in the picture.

As I look back on my childhood, I have many good memories of relatives who went out of their way to care about me and be interested in what I was doing. I remember an elderly unmarried great aunt by marriage, Aunt Jo, and an older widow, Cousin Minnie, both of whom were a pleasure to meet and be with. Even though both my widowed grandmothers went beyond the call of duty in every way (one was an intrepid tourist and we had all kinds of expeditions to strange and exciting places), I somehow felt that they owed it to us to be kind. But Minnie and Jo didn't. They were single people who had decided to be part of things and they belonged. They were interested in others, although their own lives were lived within limited horizons. It is worth noting that as a child I don't remember thanking them especially. But they knew I loved them.

Interests

It is one of the anomalies of a fallen world that couples with children feel depressed because most of their leisure time goes into the care and education of their children. Single people complain that they have no children to care for and don't know what to do with their leisure time. I would always encourage couples to have some interest beyond their own home, however satisfying it may be. To a greater degree the single person needs to cultivate interests that are intelligent, enriching and, if possible, helpful to others. A productive hobby like woodworking or needlework adds a touch of color to one's life.

I have always thought hobbies were a waste of time and a reason for going to purgatory. Some, in fact, are (e.g., collecting different ginger ale bottle tops). A good hobby, such as painting, is an opportunity for self-expression. It may reveal to a person the treasures of life which we seldom recognize. In recent years I have found amateur astronomy a fascinating pastime which I share with many other people. It is also a productive source of meditation and prayer.

The best interest of all is people. We have already spoken about friendship and intimacy. Close friends are part of the richness of life. Cardinal Newman is said to have remarked that the greatest blessing he had received was that he had good friends. We have seen that friendship means the sharing of non-sexual intimacy based on complementarity, community of interest and experience, or perhaps differences. It is worthwhile having friends of different backgrounds and interests as long as some things, such as values, can be shared.

It is also very rewarding to have friends of different ages. A good collection of friends includes older people who serve as mentors, or at least as observers of the passing scene. A few young friends can keep you from getting old. There is nothing more refreshing than learning from an older friend or passing on treasures to a younger one. This fulfills for a single person many of the needs that we all feel, namely, the impulse to be children at one time and parents at another.

In addition to intimate friends, we need interesting and friendly acquaintances. The single person should mix with the well-known and also with the quiet and private type. Most of the time we can find someone who is well known and sparks life into things without being intrusive. We may get to be friends with such a person. This should be balanced with friendly relations with the barber, the shoemaker, and the lady at the deli. A few words exchanged regularly on the street, an act of kindness, a call to offer a prayer at the wake of the postman's wife—all these things make life worth living, especially for the single. If you take the time to be interested in people, your worst problem will be trying to control your Christmas card list.

Better To Love and Lose

Whether a person is married or single, there are always new opportunities to be generous beyond the call of duty. They come more readily to the single who is presumed, not always accurately, to have more resources. For example, a nephew from a large family may need an advanced college-placement fee of a few hundred dollars; a second cousin in unfortunate circumstances could use some extra money to defray the cost of the reception at her upcoming wedding; one's sister may be trying to get a down payment on a house. In all these cases people look to the single person. He or she should try to look back, with a helping hand.

Many single people resent these expectations; in fact, single people pay a higher percentage of taxes as individuals than do married people, and, indeed, it costs almost as much for one person to live as it does for two. Nor does anyone remember that a single person has to provide completely for his or her old age.

If, however, you would like to live life to its fullest, it is a good principle to give until it hurts a bit, even if others forget your generosity. Relatives and friends may never think of paying you back when their ship comes in, but it is better to love and lose than not to have loved at all. We are told in the Gospel to imitate our heavenly Father who is generous to all. The stingy person not only fails to let others in, but also fails to let God in. If a single person lacks a sense of generosity, he or she is sure to have other problems in life—a lonely pleasure or a scarlet letter.

The Restless Heart

In Chapter 6 we will discuss the single person's spiritual life. We will consider chaste celibacy as an essential component in the spiritual development of the unmarried person. Here a word needs to be said in the context of being single with style.

In the *Confessions,* St. Augustine prayed, "You have made us for Yourself, O God, and our hearts are restless until they rest in You." The single person who does not lead a vibrant spiritual life, with resolution and a willingness to persevere in trial and aridity, is going to experience a terribly restless heart. The man with a family may find some consolation in knowing that he serves God by serving his wife and children. Even if he is secretly unchaste and unfaithful in spite of good intentions and love for his wife, he can console himself with the knowledge that he has "put the bread on the table." The single person, however, even a cleric or religious, enduring loneliness, misunderstanding and perhaps moral failure, must face all this alone. Friends are great but they are not always there, especially in the dead of night.

For the single person, the answer is a dedicated and ordered life of prayer. This includes frequent participation in the Eucharistic liturgy and reception of the sacraments. Devotion to Christ in the Eucharist is the emotional center in the lives of many single people. Habits of daily prayer, spiritual reading, and regular meditation have become a part of the rhythm of life. A good regime of prayer can be established in a few weeks and it will carry a person through difficult times. The single person has no one with whom to share his or her pain and frustration, especially when sexual needs are strongly felt. It is then that prayer is so important. This is especially true for someone struggling with deviant or auto-erotic impulses.

I would like to end this chapter with a prayer by a loving, yet lonely man. Francis Thompson was separated from his family, and in many ways unsuccessful in his personal life, although he was a great poet. He searched throughout his life and failed to do any of the things I have suggested in this chapter, but he prayed and thanked God. He wrote this poem by Charing Cross bridge in London, where he used often to sit on the park benches near the Thames Embankment. Perhaps some of the strength this lonely man derived from the presence of Christ will come to you as you read these few lines.

The Kingdom of God

'In no Strange Land'
O world invisible, we view thee,
O world intangible, we touch thee,
O world unknowable, we know thee,
Inapprehensible, we clutch thee!

Does the fish soar to find the ocean,
The eagle plunge to find the air—
That we ask of the stars in motion
If they have rumour of thee there?

Not where the wheeling systems darken,
And our benumbed conceiving soars!—
The drift of pinions, would we hearken,
Beats at our own clay-shuttered doors.

The angels keep their ancient places;—
Turn but a stone, and start a wing!
'Tis ye, 'tis your estrangèd faces,
That miss the many-splendoured thing.

But (when so sad thou canst not sadder)
Cry;—and upon thy so sore loss
Shall shine the traffic of Jacob's ladder
Pitched betwixt Heaven and Charing Cross.

Yea, in the night, my Soul, my daughter,
Cry,—clinging Heaven by the hems;
And lo, Christ walking on the water
Not of Gennesareth, but Thames!

6

The Dark Side and the Light Side

In some respect, the last chapter was the easiest to write and this is the most difficult, because it deals with so many things which are apparently irrational and make no easy sense. Yet this is perhaps the most important chapter for understanding chaste celibacy and for successfully leading a chaste life. Fantasies, dreams, temptations, and sins form the dark side of the picture; they are often mysterious and cause intense suffering for the individual. The light or bright side is the successful achievement of chastity, whether in a single incident of temptation, or over a period of time, or for life. We must take a careful, intelligent look at both the dark and the bright sides.

Fantasies

All aspects of life are reflected in some way in the conscious mind. We are aware, albeit faintly, of biological functions in our body, but they are so persistent that we are not likely to avert to them consciously until they stop, or are impaired. We come to notice a clock only when it has stopped ticking. We are often made aware of our unfulfilled needs by memories of their fulfillment in the past or by desire and fantasy in the present. Some who have lived through near starvation have later recalled that they had fantasies of eating meals, which were mostly remembered from previous good times. Sexual fantasies reflect not only our biological drives but also such deeply felt needs as the sexual expression of one's own being, and the need for tenderness, reinforcement, intimacy and spiritual love.

Fantasy may or may not be a voluntary phenomenon. Usually it is involuntary at first, flowing from the whole organism and emerging from its need to put all experience into a single frame of experience or *gestalt*. Fantasy becomes voluntary when it is accepted and fomented by desire. This happens when a person is writing a novel and making up a story.

Sexual fantasy is always involuntary at first and simply reflects the various levels of need of the individual. If it is accepted and augmented, it becomes more or less voluntary. The mandate to avoid evil desires, given by Christ in the Sermon on the Mount (see Mt 5:28-29), requires that we not indulge voluntarily and knowingly in forbidden sexual desires. Such desires can result from sexual fantasy voluntarily entertained. The moral significance here does not come from the fantasy itself, but from the person's desire and the circumstances. For instance, it is not morally wrong for a married man to fantasize about proper sexual relations with his wife when she is absent.

Frequently single people report very active sexual fantasies and are concerned that they may be sinful. A careful distinction must be made here. No one has much control over the force of fantasy because, as mentioned above, it represents the needs and drives which well up in the mind (psyche) and the body of the individual. One cannot stop the tides, but they can be controlled.

In the case of strong sexual fantasies, it seems unrealistic to deny some modicum of voluntary acceptance of them in the conscious mind. It must be determined, however, whether there has been a voluntary admission of fantasy; if so, the deed is culpable. To be culpable, or sinful, such an admission must be reflective as well as voluntary. The person must have the presence of mind to say consciously, "This is wrong, but I am going to think about it anyway." If the person has been struggling with sexual feelings and fantasies for some time (and sexual need appears to ebb and flow), even such a statement may be made at a time of distraction and without full responsibility.

Is there an easy rule of thumb to determine whether there has
been moral consent to sexual fantasy and forbidden desire? It
seems to me that the best practical test for this is to answer the
following questions:

1. Did I voluntarily augment or add to the fantasy?
2. Did I respond to it in a physical way, either by voluntary sexual
   arousal or by some action in pursuit of augmenting the fantasy,
   e.g., by looking at stimulating objects on purpose?
3. When I became aware of what I was doing, did I refuse to turn
   my attention to something else?

If the answer to *all* these questions (especially the last) is clearly
and unequivocally *yes*, then I think the person is culpable. Even
this full culpability may be reduced by other factors related to the
person or situation. Without a "yes" answer to these questions I
would presume that a sincere person has done nothing morally
wrong. It is a good rule to remember that serious sin cannot be
committed accidentally. Psychologically serious sin is an awesome
occasion in the life of a struggling Christian.

In other ages these questions and conclusions might have seemed
lax and unwarranted. However, our norms for judging these things
must be founded on a sound understanding of human behavior.
The simple fact is that people don't have that much control over
fantasy. You may have observed this if you have tried to follow a
boring lecture, or to pray in a distracting situation.

Suppose a person becomes very adept at controlling fantasy,
especially sexual fantasy. This need not be the best adjustment,
because such control may suggest the use of repression, a defense
mechanism which unconsciously buries drives, needs and
spontaneous desires, and triggers the beginning of fantasy in the
unconscious. It is likely that a reservoir of repressed sexual
material will be stored up which could lead to uncontrollable
acting out in the future. Many sad cases of the effects of repression
and the loss of control dot the pages of history. Most behavioral
scientists accept it as a fact that repression is always incomplete

and inadequate. The repressed person is bound to lose control in the future and suffer serious effects in the present.

Conscious control is quite different from repression. By definition, the person is aware of turning away, or at least of not augmenting a fantasy or desire. He is not trying to stop the tide but simply to control it, so as not to be swept away. When we discuss anxiety later, we will see its close relationship to fantasy, and how high levels of anxiety may precipitate acting out behavior which leads to sin.

Temptation

When we speak of fantasy, we are using the language of psychology. Temptation, on the other hand, is a theological term and may be defined as an invitation to do something wrong, or something that is in itself good but not in the present circumstances. To be real, a temptation must elicit a response of desire on the part of the one tempted. There are many things that are forbidden, such as robbing a bank, but few of us have been tempted to do them.

I have noticed that when people say they have asked for the grace of chastity, they have frequently asked for the grace to be an angel—a grace they will not receive. It is not that they don't want to sin; they don't want to be tempted.

Temptation has its origin both in the mind, with the desires and needs we have spoken of, and in the body, with its systems which seek release or fulfillment. Religiously motivated people will often include the Prince of Darkness among their sources of temptation, and far be it from me to deny that possibility. However, we have quite enough equipment—psychological and biological—to account for most of our temptations. I suspect that when a reasonably mature person who is trying seriously to be a good Christian encounters very strong or overpowering sexual temptations, there is either a mismanagement of the environment leading to extreme anxiety or an unresolved inner conflict expressing itself in a sexual way.

Does this excuse the individual from struggling with temptation, or absolve him of all responsibility? There is no lack of popular religious books that give this impression; however, I could not disagree more. My disagreement arises from a knowledge of Catholic moral theology and the writings of the spiritual masters. It has been corroborated, moreover, by my many interviews with people who have followed the easy way suggested by popular writers and found themselves in the grip of sexual habits, which they knew from experience were morally wrong and damaging to their personal and spiritual growth. Powerful temptations may indeed reduce responsibility, and the recognition of this fact may allow a person to forgive himself more easily and move on. Such temptations, however, give no permission to sin, or, what is worse, to pretend that sin is not sin.

Temptation is part of life and clear and consistent evidence of the mystery of original sin. The desire to be without temptation is part of the unrealism which so many therapists have come to see as a root of sexual problems. Temptation can be an excellent teacher; it can act like a sparring partner to a boxer. Throughout Sacred Scripture and religious history all those who sought God struggled with temptation, and any number of them frequently fell and repented. Most important, temptation teaches us that we cannot save ourselves, that we must rely on the power of God and the saving grace of His Son, or else we will be lost. To turn from Him is to perish; to turn toward Him is to live.

Even if you follow all the suggestions in this book, straighten out your life in a healthy way, work on your spiritual life and are faithful to prayer and the sacraments, a day may still come when you are tempted beyond what you expected or think you can endure. At that point you will learn the effect of the gifts of the Holy Spirit, which, after your fiercely painful hour, will lift you on eagle's wings. Only then will it be clear to you what it means to be saved. The hour of trial may come many times. You may fail or

succeed, and it will come again and again. If you succeed, you will
grow, and in growing you will become a blessing to others in ways
that you could not foresee in the dark hour of temptation.

The Temptation of Temptation

To prepare for the hour of trial it is best to overcome less powerful
and virulent temptations. Every temptation that is overcome
strengthens a person, even if there are subsequent failures. The
most dangerous temptation for those trying to be chaste is what I
call the "temptation of temptation."

The tempted person's mind is in a state of conflict. It is a painful
time when the individual is pulled in opposite directions. He or
she has little or no inner peace, is anxious about the immediate
future, apprehensive concerning spiritual danger, and angry and
frustrated over such a conflict. Then the temptation of temptation
comes: "Oh, get it over with! What difference will one more
episode make. Then I will be at peace or at least able to pray with
repentance. God will seem near, whereas He seems so far away
now."

If there is any place in sexual temptation where I am inclined to
see the effects of the diabolical, it is precisely in this almost pious
suggestion. The antidote to this enticement is to recall that every
temptation resisted is a great act of worship of God. To put up with
temptation and not seek the easy way out is a powerful
acknowledgment of the sovereignty of God and of Christ, our
lawgiver and king. Resisting temptation means seeking first the
kingdom of God. Even if one falls later on, he has accomplished an
act of obedient worship that will not be erased.

Anxiety

Anxiety, which begins in the individual's body and mind,
generates an apprehension of danger and destruction. It can cause
a distortion of the vital force which keeps us alive. To live and
grow we must struggle to go beyond our fears and apparent

limitations. When this impulse to struggle and move on becomes blocked by fear and apprehension, the result is neurotic anxiety. A manageable level of normal anxiety is often necessary for concentrated action and it dispels distractions. As Samuel Johnson once observed, there is nothing that will concentrate one's attention better than the knowledge that one is to be hanged next Tuesday. Serious people, such as those who read books on chastity, frequently have an excess of anxiety. St. Paul's daily pressing care for all the churches may be an example. Despite our Savior's frequent admonitions not to worry, we love to worry, and when we worry we tap reservoirs of anxiety deep within us. If being a disciple makes you anxious, you cannot blame the Master in this case.

Now, don't feel bad. If you decided to throw it all overboard and be a sinner, you would be just as anxious as you are now and you would have the added anxiety of being alienated from God. I've observed that Christians who gave up their faith and took the short route to the flesh pots are invariably flops as sinners. Instead of enjoying to the limit the short-lived pleasures of the world, they spend much of their time eagerly trying to induce others to follow them. Like Don Quixote they end up sparring with church steeples rather than with windmills. Ex-Christians make very unconvincing sinners indeed, as we see in the troubled life of James Joyce, or in that of Aubrey Beardsley, the artist of the obscene who anxiously made it back to God in time to receive the last rites of the Church.

Anxiety does not come from being a believer or trying to be a disciple, but it does interfere with the believer's resisting temptation and accepting God's will. The following suggestions are intended to help those in a state of anxious temptation. They come from various people I have known over the years who have become expert at overcoming temptation.

1. Calm down and recognize consciously (say it yourself) that you are being seriously tempted and should take appropriate

measures. A walk around the block, a quiet time sitting and relaxing in church or in your room will do a world of good.

2. Ask yourself what the sources of this particular temptation are. Our considerations in previous chapters may provide some clues. Are there specific reasons that you are anxious, depressed, lonely, etc.? Have you tried to remedy them? What should you do right now?

3. Gently call upon God for some inner peace and make an act of confidence in Him.

4. Do something else. Temptation cannot occur when one is occupied; therefore, step out of the present scene as dramatically as you can. Call a friend, go to the movies, get involved with someone else's problems. Calling the police or throwing a pie at someone may be a bit much, but some activity that breaks the pattern of your present situation is called for. It's amazing how few people are tempted to sin during a fire alarm.

Falls

If a person is still spiritually weak, or does not have his life in good order, or is still struggling with a compulsion which he is trying to overcome, he is likely to fall. It takes about three months to reduce substantially the pull of a habit. Many people find it difficult even to get to that three months of abstinence where it gets easier. In overcoming a sexual compulsion, any kind of forbidden voluntary sexual behavior, including auto-eroticism, tends to reinforce the original compulsion. Three months means three months of chastity.

A fall or the possibility of a fall, therefore, becomes part of the struggle for those who are trying to lead a chaste life. One of Christ's great gifts to His children is the knowledge that forgiveness is as close as a prayer and a good resolution. The sacrament of reconciliation, with the very valuable and therapeutic experience of verbal confession, is a most powerful sign of Christ's forgiveness. The prayer of perfect contrition, that is, of sorrow out of love for God, coupled with the resolution to try to sin no more, is also a very effective tool in the spiritual life. Such prayer should be said often and should culminate in the celebration of the sacrament. It is dangerous and unwise to delay the act of perfect contrition.

Paradoxically those trying to be chaste may be contrite in one way, and yet they may actually continue to perform the sinful act. They wish to God that this was not happening to them. This confusion is a sure sign of compulsion. As soon as the person who falls has regained his or her balance, prayer is the next step. The more trusting and loving the prayer can be, the more effectively it can calm the individual. The words of Christ to St. Peter can be very significant at this point: "Satan has got his wish to sift you all like wheat, but I have prayed for you, Simon, that your faith may not fail, and once you have recovered, you in your turn must strengthen your brother" (Lk 22:32-33).

Falls make for contrition, and contrition produces greater love of God. If a person can face temptations and falls (tragic though they be) with prayer and confession, they can become a powerful source of repentance.

Contrition and Guilt

In putting falls to work for chastity, it is most important that the contrition is not simply the expression of neurotic guilt. The following quotation from Meister Eckhart, the thirteenth-century German mystic, shows a great deal of psychological insight into the difference between neurotic guilt and real contrition.

> Repentance is of two kinds; one is of time and of the senses, the other is divine and supernatural. Repentance in time always declines into greater sorrow and plunges a man into lamentation, as if he must now despair; and there repent-

ance remains in its sorrow, and can make no progress; nothing comes of it.

But divine repentance is quite different. As soon as a man has achieved self-loathing, at once he lifts himself up to God, and establishes himself in an eternal turning away from all sin in an immovable will; and there he lifts himself up in great confidence to God, and achieves a great security. And from this there comes a spiritual joy that lifts the soul up out of all sorrow and lamentation, and makes it secure in God. For the weaker a man finds himself and the more have been his misdeeds, the more cause he has to bind himself to God with an undivided love in which there is no sin or weakness. Therefore the best path up which a man proceeds, when he wants to go to God in all devotion, is for him to be sinless, made strong by a godly repentance.

And the heavier a man's sins are as he weighs them, the readier is God to forgive them, and to come to the soul, and to drive the sins out. Every man does his utmost to get rid of what most irks him. And the greater and the more the sins are, still immeasurably more is God glad and ready to forgive them, because they are irksome to him. And then, as godly repentance lifts itself up to God, sins vanish into God's abyss, faster than it takes me to shut my eyes, and so they become utterly nothing, as if they had never happened, if repentance is complete.[1]

Dreams

The understanding and use of dreams can be of great importance in leading a chaste life. Dreams are experiences which permit the unconscious to rise to the surface of the mind; they also allow certain involuntary expressions of a sexual nature to occur in sleep. The first encounter most people have with sexuality is likely to be in a pre-pubescent dream. For a person who decided at an early age to lead a chaste life, dreams present an important opportunity

---

1. *Meister Eckhart*, trans. Edmund Colledge, O.S.A. and Bernard McGinn. New York: Paulist Press, 1982 (Classics of Western Spirituality), pp. 262–63.

for psychological maturation. This stems from the fact that the dream experience may bring symbolically to the person's mind and memory levels of development, of which he or she would have been otherwise unaware. There is probably no group of people for whom dreams are more important than maturing celibates.

In contemporary psychological theories of consciousness, dreams are thought to have their origin in memory traces, templates and engrams (memory units) which are woven into percept-like experiences during sleep or semi-sleep. (We say percept-like, because dreams are not real perceptions.) In this respect dreams are akin to hallucinations. The mind has a tendency to weave the strands of thought and memory into a single coherent field or *gestalt*. When this occurs, a dream will have a sequence and coherent parts, although these will not be controlled by reason or by our knowledge of objective reality, but by unconscious impulses.[2] For this reason dreams can often exhibit in symbolic ways not only conscious concerns and memories, but also deeply repressed (and unconscious) needs and desires.

When a person has refrained on purpose from expressing or even delving into sexual needs in order to avoid conscious sexual arousal when awake, it is logical that this arousal and the needs and desires causing it will be expressed in dreams. Since most dreams seem to occur during light sleep, it is quite possible to remember dreams vividly. The more complex the dream is, the more it appears to represent needs, interests and even conflicts which the person is experiencing in conscious life. During semi-sleep there may occur a hypnogogic hallucination—an experience much like a dream insofar as it is not under the individual's voluntary control. Unlike other hallucinations it is not related to mental illness or to the use of hallucinogenic drugs.

---

2. L.J. West, "A General Theory of Hallucinations and Dreams," in *Hallucinations,* ed. L.J. West. New York: Grune & Stratton, 1962. For a more popular discussion of dreams and their relation to the spiritual life, cf. Morton Kelsey, *God, Dreams and Revelation.* Minneapolis: Augsburg Publishing House, 1974 (originally published as *Dreams the Dark Speech of the Spirit.* Garden City: Doubleday, 1968), Chapter 9.

It is my impression that those who have a sexual dream or fantasy when half-awake, or even a vivid non-psychotic hallucination, may experience a good deal of guilt. The experience is so vivid that they feel they must have been responsible. I would like to do everything possible to dispel this illusion, which I believe has caused discouragement and neurotic guilt for many sincere Christians. Guilt in turn can express itself in conscious forbidden behavior. Pascal warned the spiritual that if they try to be angels, they might become beasts.

Since dreams and dreamlike states have no moral consequences, can relieve a great deal of sexual tension, and possibly reduce biological drives after sleep, I believe that dreams should be carefully understood. This is especially true for those trying to lead a chaste celibate life. It might almost be said, with a touch of irony, that sexual dreams are a byproduct of chastity, since they are not as likely to occur if sexual release is part of the conscious life of the individual.

In the past when dreams were not understood, the devout often went to great lengths to try to prevent sexual dreams: they would sleep on boards or on a narrow cot, immerse themselves in cold streams, and sprinkle their bed with holy water before retiring. All of this may have been counterproductive.

Therapists have discovered that if a person consciously suggests that he dream, he will do so more frequently and remember his dreams better. Thus we can suggest to ourselves to dream, and, if the dream wakes us, to fall back to sleep. We can suggest getting up at a particular hour or when some faint sound is heard. Frequently this works without an alarm clock. The appropriate suggestion can also be made not to wake up, if we know that another person is leaving the house early.

I recommend that those who foresee the possibility of sexual dreams, because of a day of temptation or persistent fantasies, suggest to their own psyche that they continue to sleep or return to sleep if sexual arousal or release occurs. To do otherwise might be a rather puritanical rebellion against the laws of nature in the name of angelism. We have already mentioned that God has apparently not been very cooperative with those who have tried to become angels. On the other hand, an overly permissive attitude toward dreams may mask an indulgence of voluntary sexual arousal. The counsel of a wise confessor is necessary in such cases.

The content of dreams can often provide great opportunities for insight. The secret is to look for the meaning hidden beneath the dream symbolism. For instance, sexual dreams usually indicate a strong desire to love and be loved in return. A person may be startled by the sexual symbolism but cope quite well with the idea that he or she desires to be loved. The presence of strong sexual desires in dreams also denotes that a great deal of repression may already have taken place and may be continuing. While the analysis of dreams is a complex study and requires considerable training, a thoughtful person may derive insight into the subconscious mind. But to do this it is essential to go beyond the dream symbolism that is usually provided by the memory of conscious fantasies which occurred while awake.

Coping with Success

The chaste celibate must cope not only with failure but also with success. For some, success at being chaste may have lasted for many years, or perhaps a lifetime. Others will have persevered in chastity only a short while. The great danger of success in practicing any virtue is pride—the belief that one has done it on one's own or with just "a little help from above." While such an attitude may not lead to a sexual fall, it certainly does not enhance one's perception of the spiritual reality of salvation.

Successes may also make a person less cautious in two ways. If one is inclined to puritanism, success can lead to more rigidly puritanical ideas, since these appear to work so well. If the individual has been careless in arranging a healthy life-style, he may take even less care now. On the other hand, if one has been rather liberal in expressing affection and has formed unwise relationships, he may continue on the same road until the serious fall occurs. Success can easily become a danger.

Despite the cautionary advice and pitfalls, both obvious and subtle, the goal we have set for ourselves in this book is to lead a chaste life successfully. With grace and good will this goal is achieved sooner or later. Invariably the achievement brings with it a profound sense of humility, and the awareness that we carry our treasure in vessels of clay. Success in maintaining or achieving chastity without the use of repression is almost always accompanied by a growing understanding of, and compassion for, those who are obviously having great difficulties with their sexual lives.

When a person's efforts to be chaste are continually realized, something quite beautiful happens—something that has to be experienced to be appreciated. There is not only a sense of accomplishment, but also a growing awareness of Christ's presence and of intimacy with Him in the soul. As it says in St. Bernard's hymn, *Jesu Dulcis Memoria,* only one who has experienced this can believe it.

Again I have recourse to St. Augustine to find an apt expression of this experience of Christ. His prayer of thanksgiving after his conversion is filled with a captivating sense of the spiritual presence of Christ.

> O Lord, *I am Thy servant; I am Thy servant and the son of Thy handmaid. Thou hast broken my bonds. I will sacrifice to Thee the sacrifice of praise.* Let my heart and my tongue praise Thee, and *let all my bones say: O Lord, who is like to Thee?* Let them say and do Thou answer me and say to my soul: *I am Thy salvation.* Who am I and what kind of man am I? What evil has there not been in my deeds or if not in my deeds, in my words, or if not in my words then in my will? But You, Lord, are good and merciful, and Your right hand had regard to the profundity of my death and drew out the abyss of corruption that was in the bottom of

my heart. By Your gift I had come totally not to will what I willed but to will what You willed. But where in all that long time was my free will, and from what deep sunken hiding place was it suddenly summoned forth in the moment in which I bowed my neck to Your easy yoke and my shoulders to Your light burden, Christ Jesus, my Helper and my Redeemer? How lovely I suddenly found it to be free from the loveliness of those vanities, so that now it was a joy to renounce what I had been so afraid to lose. For You cast them out of me, O true and supreme Loveliness, You cast them out of me and took their place in me, You who are sweeter than all pleasure, yet not to flesh and blood; brighter than all light, yet deeper within than any secret; loftier than all honour, but not to those who are lofty to themselves. Now my mind was free from the cares that had gnawed it, from aspiring and getting and weltering in filth and rubbing the scab of lust. And I talked with You as friends talk, my glory and my riches and my salvation, my Lord God."[3]

---

3. *Confessions*, IX-I, *op. cit.*, p. 143.

7

Chastity and Spirituality

Long before the preaching of the Gospel, chaste celibacy and
chaste discipline in marriage had been linked with spirituality in
many world religions. In the Orient monks and nuns observed
religious celibacy long before the Christian era. In some world
religions even the married were expected to observe sexual
abstinence at sacred times, especially during periods of religious
initiation. Even today married Buddhists may become monks for
several months. The reason for this discipline may have been more
anthropological than spiritual, but the fact remains that man has
historically linked sexual abstinence with the search for God.

In the Christian world the idea of a chaste celibate life springs
from the Gospels and the Pauline writings. The concept was an
integral part of the early Church even before the establishment of
the first monastic communities at the end of the persecutions.
Despite the long Christian tradition of the celibate life, an
individual who is faced with the prospect of being single and
chaste may not immediately realize the implications of his situation
in terms of the spiritual journey to God. The opportunity for
chaste celibacy may come from a call to apostolic commitment or
from a marriage that ends in divorce. More than one penitent—
such as St. Margaret of Cortona—has arrived at a chaste life after
having been someone's mistress. However one reaches the state of
celibacy, it can be a great help in finding God. It is worthwhile to
explore the relationship between the struggle to be chaste and the
search for God.

Service

In his letter of Holy Thursday, 1980, to bishops and priests, Pope John Paul II offered celibacy as an imitation of Christ the Good Shepherd who spent Himself for His flock. The Holy Father suggested that celibacy made priests more available to serve others. If we apply his words to any celibate Christian and join them to the obligation of Christ's followers to be people of generous service who are open to opportunities for charity and love, then we see how celibacy can be part of any single Christian's vocation.

This is not to deny that Christian marriage also offers the opportunity to be open and generous. But the celibate Christian, religious or lay, is called in a special way to be a brother or sister to others, a generous friend and a willing help in time of need. In the past many single people have done just this, with little or no recognition that theirs was a special Christian service stemming from their vocation. Such service is more likely to be recognized as part of the vocation of a priest or religious, but that does not make it any easier to give this service.

The Life of Prayer

Some years ago a woman called me for an appointment. I explained to her that I only see clergy because the press of time limited me to that responsibility, but she insisted. She was a very intelligent professional person and requested me to teach her how to pray. When I repeated my policy about seeing only clergy, she said, "I knew you would not help me. I heard you were anti-gay." I replied that she had heard wrong if she thought I was against "gay" people, but if she had heard that I was opposed to genital homosexual behavior, she was right.

In spite of the misunderstanding, she had challenged me to help her and I agreed to a few meetings to discuss prayer over a year's time. I never alluded to her statement on homosexuality again. At the end of the sessions she told me of her decision to live a chaste life and was preparing to take a vow of chastity as a member of a lay community. She asked me to attend the ceremony. I was astonished. She explained that prayer had become so meaningful to her that her former life-style had become quite distasteful. She had found God and peace in prayer, she said, and had no desire to threaten her new happiness by returning to a life of sexual indulgence. She was not sure that a chaste life was the answer for others in her situation, but she was certain that it was for her.

A life of prayer is a very serious commitment. At first it means fidelity to meditation and vocal prayer, but as time goes on it leads to inner purification and a more intense listening to the promptings of the Holy Spirit. It takes much discipline to get started. That discipline and the desire for greater spiritual growth can coexist with serious moral falls only during the period of struggle. After a time, however, a person who has not achieved the moral integration which the Gospel and the saints insist on will grow tired of prayer and give up any real search for God.

On the other hand, anyone who has taken to heart the admonition, "If you love me, keep my commandments" (Jn 14:15), will start to grow in prayer even if there are falls, which one deeply regrets. This development both requires and elicits a growing faith and trust in God. These, in turn, bring the individual beyond the elementary forms of prayer.

As the person makes progress, he or she may experience contemplative meditation. This is much more of a gift than an achievement, and it requires great inner peace and a silencing of the tumultuous strivings of the flesh. As the person is drawn on, chastity and, in fact, the rejection of all deliberate sin becomes imperative. Prayer is seen as the pearl of great price and the treasure hidden in the field. Mature Christian prayer is the profound psychological realization of the kingdom of God within.[1]

---

1. Dr. Morton Kelsey and John Sanford have done some very interesting research on the idea of the kingdom of God within and its use by the Fathers of the Church, based on Luke 17:21. Cf. Morton Kelsey, *Companions on the Inner Way.* New York: Crossroad, 1983, p. 48.

In my book *Listening at Prayer*, I have noted that Catholic spiritual writers have always recognized personal devotion to Jesus Christ as a positive help in growth in virtue. Naturally, the devotion is centered on the Eucharistic Presence of Christ in a most positive way. My own experience has demonstrated the necessity of such devotion for a chaste life. No matter where a person is on the spiritual journey, this devotion is both relevant and healing. (For most Catholics the same can be said about devotion to Our Lady.)

A few years ago a very fine Protestant clergyman came to see me about a problem of anonymous homosexual contacts. He was married and had a family which he cherished deeply. The problem of homosexual behavior had come into his life only in his thirties, and he was deeply troubled by it. Not only was it sinful, but he was terrified that he might infect his wife with some disease. He had prayed, fasted and made a retreat.

After a few sessions I mentioned to him that a number of Catholics have found a daily hour spent in prayer before the Blessed Sacrament to be of great spiritual help. He was intrigued by the idea of this time spent with Christ and began to make it a part of his life. He not only gained strength against temptation but his profound guilt and self-hate began to dissipate. He came more and more to a personal acceptance of Christ's love for him. Although he had gone through the adult experience of a second conversion or "second birth," he now experienced a whole new loving awareness of Christ as his Savior.

Inner Peace

Most people who have struggled to bring chastity into their lives after a period of sexual indulgence report a remarkable experience of inner peace. The struggle may bring fearful conflict, but if the individual perseveres in chastity for several months or a year, he will experience an almost spontaneous sense of integration. The person is no longer at war with himself and, to use Augustine's powerful image, no longer suffers the gnawing anxiety of looking for sexual delight, and no longer scratches the scab of lust.[2]

People also observe a greater openness to others and less fear of manipulation (or being manipulated). A person who teaches or preaches Christ's message will do so with new enthusiasm and conviction. The history of the Church contains the stories of clergy and religious who had reformed their dissolute or lukewarm lives to become foremost apostles of Christ. Although it is not said, it is my impression that it was the sexual reform of their lives which provided them with the energy and clear vision to work as they had not been able to do before.

It is important to mention here that we are not speaking only about sublimation of sexual energy. Sublimation is a process (at times conscious but usually unconscious) in which a person turns energy and need from one object to another which is thought to be more acceptable or noble. Indeed, much sexual energy can be sublimated in celibacy. This is true even in the case of physical energy which sexual acts require. But sublimation, in the sense that Jung uses the term, is the direction of energy to goals and aspirations which are not creations of the mind but realities which form the highest integrative functions of human nature. Clearly a chaste life should be sublimated in this sense.

The inner peace brought about by a chaste life in a fairly well-balanced person is the result of genuine, growing integration. Drawn into unity are one's beliefs, cognitive appreciation of the moral demands of faith, deeply felt religious experiences, desire for the mystical experience of grace and the gifts of the Holy Spirit, together with the vital energy of one's whole being.

Mature chastity which is based on genuine understanding and acceptance of our humanity and rooted in trust in God is a vital force that has accomplished untold good in human history. It built monasteries from Europe to Tibet; it opened and staffed countless

2. *Confessions,* IX, I.

hospitals, orphanages, and schools; it brought the Gospel to the ends of the earth. Those who disparage religiously motivated chastity display an inexcusable ignorance of the dynamics of world history, as Christopher Dawson pointed out in his book of that name.[3] Erikson whom we previously cited recognized religious celibacy as a form of generativity operating at the highest level of human development. He makes much the same point as Dawson, but from the view of developmental psychology. This power of religious chastity for good is not an abstraction in history. It is the confluence of the energies and peace of many individual lives. And your life, dear reader, can be one of those. If you are chaste, your life can bring you this great peace.[4]

In recent years many people have been helped in their spiritual lives by the form of prayer called the healing of memories.[5] This prayer form is designed to assist an individual to free self from the effects of past conflicts, hurts and failures. Memory stores the wounds of the past and brings them to mind as experiences of resentment, anger and self-hate.

In this prayer the person deliberately recalls such events and offers forgiveness to others or extends it to self. The more profoundly someone recalls the event and the more sincerely he or she offers forgiveness, the more successful the prayer is. Of course the conscious motivation for forgiveness is the individual's belief in divine mercy and the forgiving love of Christ.

---

3. *The Dynamics of World History*, ed. J.J. Mulloy. New York: Sheed & Ward, 1956. Cf. pp. 167–188.

4. When its disciplines are observed, marriage brings a similar peace. It is a sexual integration arrived at with another person. Following Catholic teaching, I maintain that there is no life-style other than marriage in which genital relations are morally acceptable. Consequently, no real moral integration is possible. What about those who claim to have found some "peace" in sexual relations outside marriage? Inner peace must be distinguished here from homeostasis, which is a psychological balance between drive and fulfillment. Both human beings and animals experience homeostasis. It is possible that a person who is going against the moral law may experience homeostasis and mistake it for inner peace for a time.

5. Those interested in this powerful form of prayer may find it helpful to read *Healing of Memories* by Dennis and Matthew Linn, S.J. (New York: Paulist Press).

It is best to perform this meditation with another person assisting in the examination of the past. The healing of memories goes beyond one's own sins or faults; it includes the memory of wrongs done to oneself and the resentment that such wrongs engendered.

There are few areas of human life which leave the individual more vulnerable than sexuality. Anger at parents, family, friends, the world and even at God may arise from sexual experiences or a lack of them. Forgiveness and faith deeply experienced may be both psychologically and spiritually therapeutic.

Love for Others

Love is an ambiguous term, which is used to describe many things: a child's dependency on parents, a young person's sexual infatuation, a parent's need to possess a child and not allow it to grow, a force that motivates someone to self-sacrifice for family and friends, or the ecstasy of a mystic's love for God. In our day when the word love is associated almost exclusively with sexuality, which in turn is identified with a form of recreation, love is not expected to be part of a celibate's life. Yet, the religious person is still expected to be compassionate but not exactly loving in a warm personal way.

It may seem surprising that St. Augustine, whose great struggle with sexual temptations was described in the previous chapters, eventually developed a whole theology of friendship and love. For him, friendship with others and with God was almost the same thing. In the *Confessions* he was able to write so beautifully about his warm friendships after his conversion, when he no longer saw chastity as the opponent of love.

Passages about marriage are often inappropriately cited from his writings to suggest that he lacked an appreciation of married love. Among the Fathers of the Church at that time, however, Augustine had a more positive attitude toward marriage than most. His critics ignore the fact that among the upper classes of the Roman Empire and in the ancient world generally, the linking of tender emotions with marriage was not a part of life as it is for us. Augustine saw half the Christian vocation as human love and friendship; the other half was friendship with God through Christ, His beloved Son.

Augustine writes: "Do you love others? Then love them in God and say to them 'Him let us love.'" His profound grief at the death of his mother and his lament for his friend Nebridius illuminate the powerful feeling of a man whose capacity to love had never been lessened by his chastity.[6]

A chaste life should gradually open a person to greater understanding and acceptance of others, especially of those who are conflicted and troubled by their own sexuality. A mature chaste person is not threatened by the sexual problems of others; he or she can be objective without being scandalized.

A chaste person should experience gradual detachment from the narcissism and self-seeking which are so easily reinforced by sexual indulgence.

A single person who is at peace should have love to share and give away. We have already seen the importance of generosity in the life of the single lay person or religious. Loving friendships with peers, with the young and the old, are not a chore for the mature celibate; they develop spontaneously. Perhaps the greatest gift of a chaste life based on love is forgiveness toward those who are jealous of the freedom and spontaneity which chastity brings. Persons who have failed to reach a decision to be chaste, either in marriage or the single life, will instinctively be jealous of the chaste person's freedom and peace. They often spend a lot of time picking the chaste apart, hoping to find some chink in their armor. Sooner or later the chaste person will achieve the confidence to go beyond such conflicts.

---

6. T.J. Van Bavel, O.S.A., *Christians in the World.* New York: Catholic Book Publishing Co., 1980. Cf. p. 31. The entire chapter on friendship can be read with profit.

Love for God

As we strive in life to be Christ's disciples, we come to realize that we do not in fact first love God; He first loves us. Chastity in married or single life is one of several spiritual struggles which reveal Christ's personal love for the individual. Patience and forgiveness are rooted in the long battle to be chaste. As we grow more and more chaste, we come to recognize Christ as the source of a spiritual delight that captivates our heart, mind, soul and spirit.

It is important to note that the freedom of thought and feeling which comes to the chaste may open wells of repressed desire and feeling. The individual may then have to face unsuspected impulses and temptations; he or she may walk along cliffs of temptation and slip into chasms of desire. It is then that the gifts of the Holy Spirit will come to rescue the traveler and carry him on.

For married and single, following God's law and the way of the Gospel leads to a blessedness that nothing else can bring. Unexpected forces of grace come into play as the person is drawn to the Divine, and the two embrace. The individual is not lost, but transformed. Even in the dark night that follows substantive spiritual progress, the pure of heart receive and respond to the gifts of the Holy Spirit. At that stage of the spiritual life, it is the gift of courage, or fortitude, that is at work in the soul. The person is able to go beyond his or her strength, and, with conscious control, to integrate long-buried, irrational forces. And out of that dark conflict which, according to the saints, accompanies every step of the spiritual journey, there comes the realization that the pure of heart do indeed see God.

Suggested Readings

If you are single, reading can and should be an important part of your life. This bibliography is not meant to be complete, but simply to suggest some books that may be helpful. An excellent bibliography for the single is to be found at the end of Susan Muto's *Celebrating the Single Life*.

In this bibliography books are arranged according to broad areas of content.

Chaste Celibacy in General

Clark, Keith, O.F.M. Cap. *An Experience of Celibacy*. Notre Dame: Ave Maria Press, 1981. A readable, practical and encouraging book on chastity, more directed toward younger religious and clergy, but helpful for anyone seeking to lead a .chaste single life.

Plé, Albert, O.P. *Chastity and the Affective Life*. New York: Herder and Herder, 1966. A serious and, at times, theological discussion of the contributions of contemporary psychology, especially Freud, and their relation to Thomistic thought. This book can be a help to a serious student of theology and psychology who needs some well-written perspectives.

Human Sexuality and Personhood—a series of papers on sexuality in general given at a workshop for American and Canadian bishops, sponsored by the Pope John Center, St. Louis.

Distributed by Franciscan Herald Press, 1434 West 51 Street, Chicago, Ill. 60609. For those interested in theoretical aspects of sexual morality.

A Chaste Life—Spiritual and Psychological Aspects

Agundo, Philomena, F.M.M. *Affirming the Human and the Holy.* Whitinsville, Mass.: Affirmation Books, 1980. A readable series of reflections inviting one to consider the possibilities of holiness in an integrated life. Like other publications of the House of Affirmation, this book can be a valuable tool for any Christian seeking to lead a chaste single life. (Write for their catalogue.)

Kraft, William. *Sexual Dimensions of Celibate Life.* New York: Andrews and McMeel, 1979. Dr. Kraft's work suggests a real understanding of the psychological aspects of religious celibacy. His extensive experience with clergy and seminarians is shared in a readable and challenging way.

Powell, John, S.J. *Why Am I Afraid To Love?* Allen, Texas: Argus Communications, 1972. Father Powell's works present serious spiritual and psychological issues in an uncomplicated way. They are especially helpful for young people.

Tyrrell, Thomas J. *Urgent Longings.* Whitinsville, Mass.: Affirmation Books, 1980. This reflective book considers many aspects of infatuation, intimacy and love from a compassionate and deeply spiritual point of view. This is not an easy task and is very well done by the author, a full-time psychotherapist with religious and clergy. This book is a *must.*

Sexual Difficulties

Harvey, John, O.S.F.S. *Pastoral Care and the Homosexual.* Catholic Information Service, Knights of Columbus, Box 1971, New Haven, Conn. 06521. A concise and informed discussion of the topic by a priest who has worked in this area for over thirty years. Although directed to pastoral workers, this booklet is helpful to anyone practically concerned with this problem. It will be sent gratis.

Moberly, Elizabeth R. *Psychogenesis—The Early Development of Gender Identity*. Boston: Routledge & Kegan Paul, 1983. This is a professional book written for those with an extensive knowledge of psychodynamic theory. The author, a research psychologist at Cambridge University, discusses trans-sexualism and homosexuality in both men and women with interesting implications for treatment.

Payne, Leanne. *The Broken Image*. Westchester, Ill.: Good News—Crossway Books, 1981. This is a powerful book of personal witness, intelligently written about the power of prayer and Gospel values in overcoming homosexual behavior. A research fellow at Yale Divinity School, Dr. Payne explodes the myth that it is impossible to do anything about homosexual difficulties. A deeply moving book for many people.

Smith, Herbert, S.J., and Dilenno, Joseph, M.D. *Sexual Inversion*. Boston: St. Paul Editions. This book by a priest and psychiatrist gives straightforward, practical answers to questions related to homosexuality, based on the teachings of the Church.

Socarides, Charles, M.D. *Homosexuality*. New York: Jason Aronson, 1978. One of the foremost psychiatrists writing on this topic gives a comprehensive review of theory and draws from his vast experience to describe effective therapy for homosexually oriented people.

Yankelovich, Daniel, *New Rules*. New York: Random House, 1981. An outstanding research psychologist gives an incisive analysis of the destructive effects of selfism in American life. Although not directly related to our topic, Professor Yankelovich identifies many problems which our culture puts in the way of a person seeking to be chaste.

Books of Spiritual Interest

Certainly every serious book on Christian spirituality contributes to a chaste life. The following books are among many that I have found useful in exploring the spiritual aspects of the struggle to be chaste.

Carretto, Carlo. *Letters from the Desert.* Maryknoll, N.Y.: Orbis Books, 1972. A book on solitude and its profound spiritual values by a Little Brother of Jesus living in the desert.

Groeschel, Benedict. *Spiritual Passages.* New York: Crossroad, 1983. In this book an attempt is made to relate the classic teachings on spirituality to contemporary developmental psychology. Many single people as well as clergy and religious claim to have found this book helpful.

Maloney, George, S.J. *Inward Stillness.* Denville, N.J.: Dimension Books, 1976. The famous Jesuit spiritual writer gives very effective insights into one of the most important positive aspects of a celibate life, interiority. This book is an invitation to make being alone a blessing.

McNamara, William, O.C.D. *The Human Adventure.* Garden City, N.Y.: Doubleday, 1974. The Carmelite founder of Nova Nada has himself proved that a celibate life can be a creative one. Tapping the sources of Christian mysticism, he makes an important statement on integrating spirituality and humanity.

Merton, Thomas. *Thoughts in Solitude.* New York: Doubleday, 1968. The value of solitude is a high priority for the single person. While all Merton's books are helpful, this one has special meaning.

Muto, Susan A. *Celebrating the Single Life.* New York: Doubleday, 1982. Required reading for anyone who is interested in living a single Christian life, by the author of the introduction to this book. Dr. Muto's own career is a testimony to the truth of her belief that a Christian life of growth in the love and knowledge of God is the most fulfilling of human experiences.

Muto, Susan A. *Blessings That Make Us Be,* New York: Crossroad, 1982. Although this decisive work on the Beatitudes is not specifically for single people, it contains many things especially appealing to clergy, religious and laity who are called to chaste celibacy.

Nouwen, Henri. *Reaching Out: The Three Movements of the Spiritual Life.* New York: Doubleday, 1975. This is a creative book on the three ways of the spiritual life, written especially for those who are not familiar with the classic theory. Even the informed will find many new insights in this very worthwhile book.

Van Kaam, Adrian, C.S.Sp. *The Transcendent Self.* Denville, N.J.: Dimension Books, 1979. This book,which is a jewel, will serve as an excellent introduction to one of the most prolific and effective writers on spirituality in America. Since the chaste celibate must struggle with the shadow and dark side of the personality, it is important to keep the transcendent side in focus. Father Van Kaam's wisdom, given in many books, is always helpful in this endeavor.

Other Additional Readings

Carnes, Patrick, Ph.D. *Sexual Addiction.* Comp Care Publications, 2415 Annapolis Lane, Minneapolis, Minn. 55441. This book by a clinical psychologist who has done extensive work with sexual addicts is a remarkable addition to the secular literature on sexual problems. Although it is not written directly from a religious point of view, its reliance on the principles of Alcoholics Anonymous gives this book a spiritual dimension that is often lacking in other works written from the perspective of secular psychology. Naturally the author does not commit himself to any denominational position, but his ideas on sexual problems are extremely helpful.

Huddleston, Mary Anne, I.H.M. (Editor) *Celibate Loving.* New York: Paulist Press, 1984. A collection of articles and essays on celibacy which are certainly interesting. Although the articles represent different points of view, the book brings together a number of interesting and helpful readings.

Kiesling, Christopher, O.P. *Celibacy, Prayer and Friendship.* New York: Alba House, 1978. A very popular book which highlights questions, feelings and decisions which occur in the celibate life. Written more from the viewpoint of a religious or priest, this book can also be a great help to the lay person.

Knight, David. *Cloud By Day, Fire By Night* (Religious Life as a Passionate Response to God). Denville, N.J.: Dimension Books, 1984.

Spirituality and Sexuality, Studies in Formative Spirituality, Vol II, No. 1, *Journal of Ongoing Formation,* Duquesne University, Pittsburgh, Pa. 15219. Several excellent articles on spirituality and sexuality are presented in this distinguished review published by the Institute of Formative Spirituality.